Friends at Court

Wimbledon and Slazenger since 1902

BRIAN SIMPSON *with* HUGH BARTY-KING

Quiller Press

ACKNOWLEDGEMENTS

Grateful acknowledgement is made to John Barrett who was a director of Slazenger and who wrote *Wimbledon, The Official History of the Championship* (Collins Willow) which is kept right up to date.

John Barrett signing up Ann Jones in 1976.

Also, Colin Dean – *Slazenger, Moss and Dean - Some Pages from a Family History.*

Professor Roy Jones of Loughborough University – research material related to the Slazenger family and the history of the Slazenger business.

Gianni Clerici – *Tennis* published by Octopus Books Limited, 1976.

Aeiner Gillmeister – *Tennis, A Cultural History* published by Leicester University Press, 1997.

Alan Little – *Wimbledon Compendium 2001*, published by The All England Tennis and Croquet Club, 2001.

Picture Acknowledgements
Front cover and page 37 – *The Times*; back cover and page 56 – All England Club; page v - Science Photo Library; page 9 – Le-Roye Productions Ltd; page 13 – The Lady magazine; page 16 – Punch magazine; page 17 – Topical Press; page 22 – National Portrait Collection; page 32 – Alfieri Picture Service; page 33 – Planet News Ltd; page 34 – Associated Press and London News Agency; page 39 – Topical Press; page 45 – The BBC; page (i), pages 46-49 (except Austin, Chambers, Connors and Borg), and pages 54-55 – Michael Cole Camerawork; page 53 – Peter Robertson

First published 2002 by Quiller Press Ltd
46 Lillie Road London SW6 1TN

ISBN 1 899163 74 3

Design and production in association with Book Production Consultants plc,
25-27 High Street, Chesterton, Cambridge, CB4 1ND, United Kingdom.
Reprographics by Colourgraphics, Cambridge, United Kingdom.
Printed by The Burlington Press, Cambridge, United Kingdom.

Contents

Foreword
by John Barrett

For organisations, as for individuals, life is a process of constant change. Nowhere has this universal truth been more apparent than at the All England Lawn Tennis and Croquet Club. Ever since the move from the original ground in Worple Road to the present site in 1922 changes and improvements have been continuous.

Recently the pace has quickened. With the implementation of the Long Term Development Plan which provided first a new No.1 Court and a state-of-the-art Broadcast Centre in 1997 and then, three years later, the magnificent Millennium Building, even regular visitors to Wimbledon have found it difficult to follow the evolutionary process.

Yet amid these bewildering changes there has been one reassuring constant. Every year the familiar green Slazenger canvas has been erected around each court. Every year the umpire's call of 'New balls please' has been the signal for ball-boys and ball-girls to open new cans of Slazenger tennis balls to service the needs of the players.

This year marks the centenary of the uninterrupted association between Slazengers and the All England Club – a remarkable testament to the quality of the product and the commitment of a company which itself has changed out of recognition since the Slazenger brothers, Ralph and Albert, first started to manufacturer rain-wear in the Manchester area during the latter half of the 19th century.

On such an occasion it is fitting that the long and romantic Slazenger story should now be told. Within these pages Brian Simpson has charted the course of events with painstaking care – events in which I was privileged to participate as a Slazenger employee for some 35 post-war years.

Working in the old London offices in Laurence Pountney Hill, a narrow lane leading down from Cannon Street towards the river, life was never dull. With so many leading cricketers, golfers, footballers, badminton, squash and hockey players – as well as tennis players – under contract it was not unusual to find in the showroom the likes of Colin Cowdrey or Denis Compton, Bobby Locke or Jack Nicklaus, Johnny Haynes or Wally Barnes, or even the entire Australian test team paying a visit in between matches.

In those days of wooden tennis rackets Stanley Barnes, the senior racket maker, was the most important man in a tennis player's life. Stanley kept each player's racket specifications on an individual card so that in his workshop – an intriguing cavern of planes, awls, vices and wood shavings with a marvellous smell of cellulose and varnish – he could produce to order frames of identical weight, balance and handle size.

During the championships each year two members of the sales team, Albert Bowler and Jack Sherwood would work in the Referee's office while a third, Peter Morgan would become the championships' 'call boy', ensuring that players due to appear on Centre Court and No.1 Court arrived on time. The practice courts in Aorangi Park were the responsibility of Czeslaw Spychala, the ever-popular former Polish Davis Cup player known by generations of home and overseas players simply as 'Spike'.

Running the championships in those amateur days was very much a family affair and the Slazenger members were a valuable part of the team. It was a relationship that prospered partly because the club and the company shared an understated style that combined flair with quality.

With the arrival of open tennis in 1968 and the subsequent appointment of professional supervisors, umpires and linesmen, the need for Slazenger representatives was reduced and eventually ended – all part of the evolutionary process.

That same process has given us this year the new Hydroguard water repellant cover on the Slazenger ball that will minimise the effect of any rain delays.

As the club moves forward towards Stage 3 of the Long Term Plan, with improvements planned for the southern end of the ground, there will doubtless be other technical innovations with the Slazenger tennis ball over the coming years that will keep it ahead of the opposition.

After 100 years of friendly co-operation between club and company it is clear that both organisations have benefited. Long may the partnership continue.

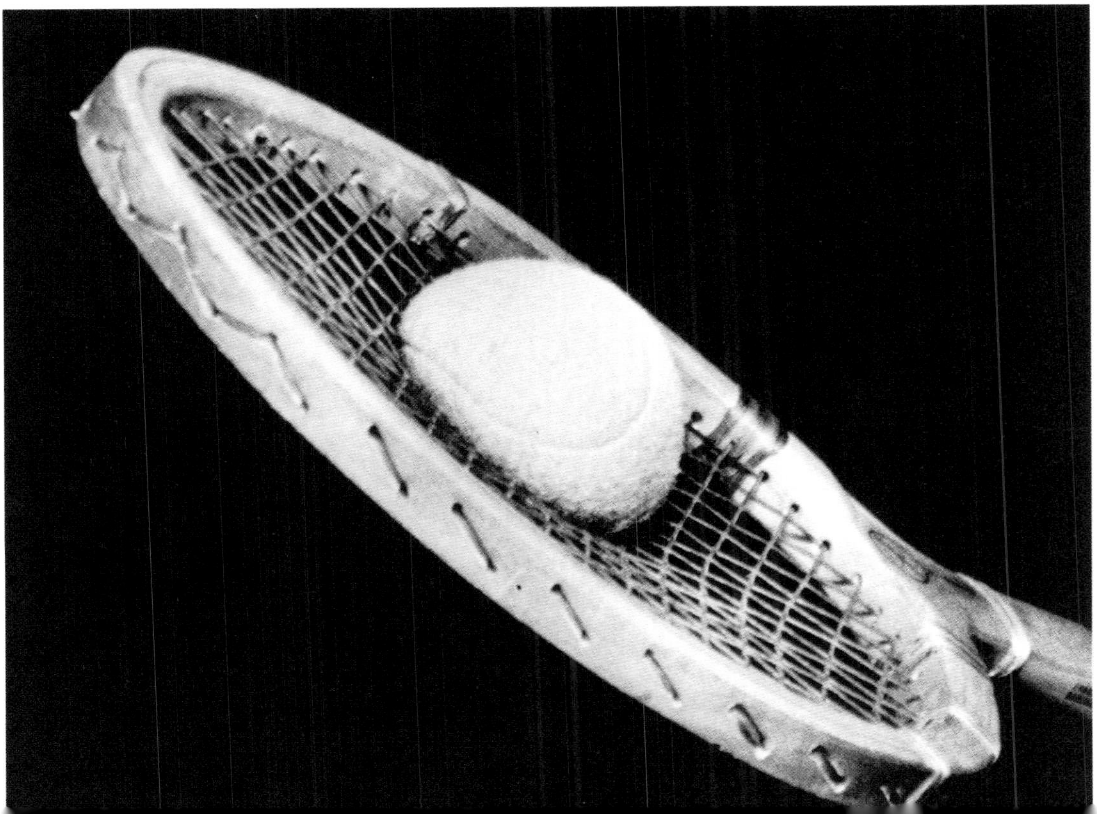

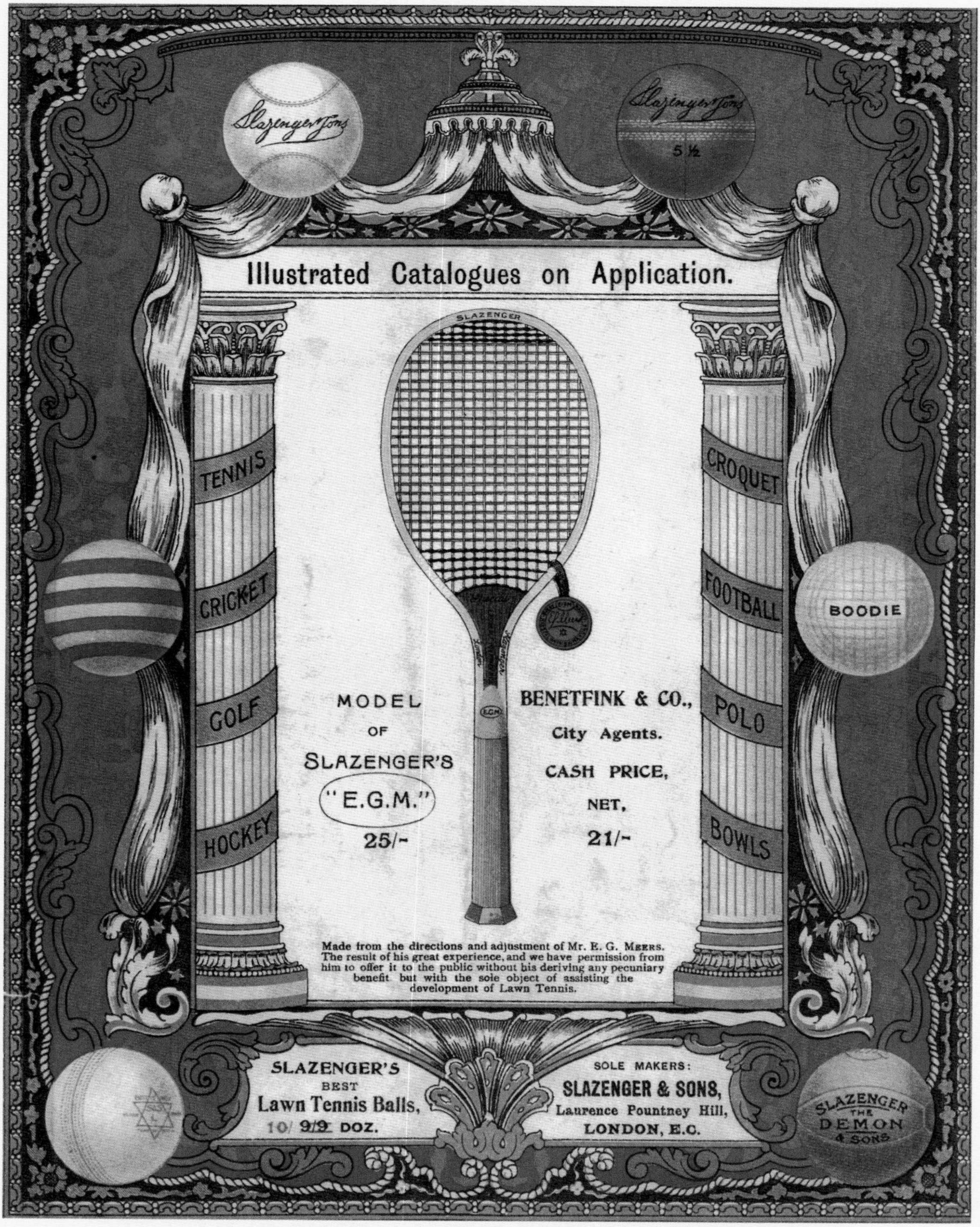

E G Meers was the expert who gave his name to Slazenger's 'EGM' racket, one of their top four frames in 1895, along with 'Demon', 'Doherty' and 'Slazenger'.

1. Warm-Up

SLAZENGER is a name which, in 2002, is known to players and watchers of the game of tennis the world over.

In the upheavals which Europe experienced at the end of the eighteenth century, families who had lived, generation after generation, in the same place, moved out to escape persecution, poverty and the harshness of a new regime which made life intolerable. When, in France, an enlightened revolution changed to Terror, French families found safety in England, as did many Polish families who hoped to become members of a more congenial society than the one Poland became after the Russians invaded in 1792, and then partitioned the country between themselves and Prussia.

On arrival in their new home, many such 'asylum seekers', as they would be called today, chose to mark their change of habitat and lifestyle by changing their names. The Jewish family who settled in Manchester at this time with the name Schlesinger, usually meaning of Silesian origins, changed it to Slazenger.

A Manchester business directory, published in 1804, included the name Mordecai Slazenger, and his address, 4 Millar's Lane. His occupation was listed as 'Umbrella Maker'. Mordecai had married an Irish girl, Isabella, and when he died in 1819 she added the more decidedly English name Moss to their surname. So, when the fourth of their six children started his working life as a second-hand clothes dealer in nearby Warrington, where he was born, it was as Joseph Slazenger Moss. In 1842 Joseph married Elizabeth Lazarus, the daughter of an itinerant trader, and within two years J S Moss and Sons had two tailor's shops, one in Warrington and another in Lancaster, combined with what was described as a woollen business trading in woollen cloth for suitings and jackets. He became a leader of the Jewish community in Manchester before he died in 1872.

He and Elizabeth had twelve children. At his death, his eldest son Ralph, who had attended Manchester Grammar School and been trained in the craft of tailoring, was 26. He took over J S Moss and Sons, and immediately acquired two more shops. By 1877 he had five of them in and around Manchester. Joining him in this flourishing family enterprise were three of his five brothers. Albert was the commercial traveller; Frank took charge of the warehouse, Horatio the shirt and hosiery side.

It was a great deal more than retailing. As his 1877 advertisement showed, J S Moss and Sons were '*makers* of four-in-hand driving coats and sporting clothing, military tailors'. With the British army and navy busy in Egypt, annexing the Transvaal and occupying Cyprus, he had no lack of customers for uniforms. But the appearance of the word 'sporting' to describe part of their activity, pointed to the direction which the main business was to take to the exclusion of all else.

Their shop at 23 Market Street, Manchester, heralded another development: 'Slazenger et Fils, importer of French fancy goods'. It was their first exercise in overseas trade – and dropped the Moss addition. In 1881 this moved to larger premises at 14, 16 and 18 Corporation Street, the city's shopping centre, and was re-registered as 'Gaiter and Legging manufacturer with factories in Manchester and Paris'.

The ship now sailed under the flag of SLAZENGER, and started the process of making the name a household word wherever tennis was talked about, played as a recreation at home or watched as a spectacle that never failed to excite and inspire.

IT STARTED INDOORS AS REAL TENNIS

The French link was a reminder of the game's origin across the Channel way back in the twelfth century as a racket and ball sport played in the courtyards of mediaeval buildings by European grandees and their royal masters, which they called *jeu de paume*. It evolved into what came to be known variously in the English speaking world as Real Tennis, Royal Tennis and Court Tennis – played in a closed space with sloping roofs and open galleries on one side and at the end. To alert his opponent that he was about to serve him a ball, the French player called 'Tenez!' – Take it! The word which echoed round the walls of the court every few minutes became so familiar a feature of the time spent on the court, that for those who played it and those who watched it, the cry became irrevocably associated with the game, to the extent that Tenez, in its anglicized form Tennis, became its name.

In Britain, Real Tennis remained an aristocratic, behind-closed-doors leisure activity for the privileged few until some ten years before Joseph Slazenger died, Major Walter Clopton Wingfield, who might well have been a customer for one of the Manchester military tailor's uniforms, thought of bringing Real Tennis out of doors and on to a grass lawn.

To the game that he can justifiably be said to have 'invented' in 1874, he gave the unwieldy name of 'Sphairistike'. Scoring was the same as in the game of Rackets. The size of the grass court varied according to the size of the lawn on which Sphairistike, a name soon dropped in favour of 'Lawn Tennis', was to be played.

Real/Royal Tennis, the forerunner of Lawn Tennis, was played by royalty with a racket, not unlike those made by Slazenger centuries later, on an indoor court flanked by open galleries.

Rackets at the Kings Bench Prison.

It was a more homely, less severe – less serious – game than Real Tennis and Rackets, unrelated to school and university 'exercise'. It was more akin to Croquet, the game for which an All England Croquet Club had been formed in 1868, leasing four acres of grass in Worple Road (now Nursery Road) Wimbledon, on which members could play croquet. When the club's committee heard of Major Wingfield's idea, they at once – in the summer of 1875 – set apart one of their croquet grounds for Sphairistike/Lawn Tennis and Badminton. Wingfield saw his court as being hour-glass shape, but the Croquet Club made theirs rectangular. On it they invited members to play a game which in most respects followed the *Laws of Lawn Tennis* which the Marylebone Cricket Club (with a Real Tennis court on their Lord's cricket ground) had issued that May.

The Croquet Club added two more tennis courts to their Worple Road site the next year, and in 1877 changed their name to 'All England Croquet and Lawn Tennis Club'. They staged a first championship meeting that July, which took its place as a major sporting event in the London Season for which the nobility and gentry left their country estates for their town houses.

The inaugural championship of 1877 was for amateur players, and consisted of one event only, Gentlemen's Singles. There was an entry of 22. The public could watch the final for a payment of one shilling. It was won by Spencer Gore, who had made a name for himself as a Rackets player as a schoolboy at Harrow. He took away 12 guineas and a silver challenge cup worth 25 guineas, which was presented by *The Field* magazine.

The All England Club took over the leadership and management of the game from the MCC, a position it retained until the formation of The Lawn Tennis Association in 1888, which was followed in 1913 by The International Lawn Tennis Federation, consisting of 13 national LTAs. Lawn Tennis was all set for changing from a social pastime of the leisure classes, as John Barrett puts it in his definitive, official history of the Wimbledon championships, into a fully fledged international sport.

MID-VICTORIAN BRITAIN PLAYED UP AND PLAYED THE GAME

In 1875, Lawn Tennis joined the many other games, indoor and outdoor – chess, backgammon, billiards, archery, rifle shooting, golf, cricket, football, hockey, boxing, rowing, bowls, to name but a few – for which, after the initial construction of the platform on which the game would be played (golf course, squash court, billiard table, soccer pitch, etc), there would be a continuing need to supply equipment and clothing on a large scale. The sports trade in Britain was now beginning to expand very rapidly.

In 1810, Edward Ayres opened a cabinet-making and wood-turning workshop in London's Clerkenwell to make equipment for the popular indoor games of the day, from which grew the broad-based sports trader F H Ayres. In 1855 H J Gray began making rackets, golf clubs and cricket bats in Cambridge, leading to the formation of H J Gray and Sons. In 1870 William Sykes, a saddler, started making leather footballs in his small shop in Horbury outside Leeds, an enterprise that was to become the extensive Yorkshire Athletic Manufactory. In 1870 Henry Gradidge opened the cricket bat works in Woolwich which was to expand into the source of a very much larger variety of sports equipment.

To all these and their many competitors, the new outlet for sports equipment that was Lawn Tennis gave hopes of a welcome increase in turnover. The eagerness with which the public seized on the new game, both to play and watch, and the willingness to pour money into the purchase of rackets, presses to clamp them in to stop warping and covers to keep them dry, 'gladstone' bags to carry them in, rubber-soled canvas shoes, eyeshades, blazers and boaters, and most important of all, boxes of tennis balls, created a vast additional market. Lawn Tennis had become the fashion.

Much of all this was bought by private 'recreational' players who would buy the clothes, rackets and balls which attracted them, and they could afford, from sports shops such as Lillywhites, the sports department of Gamages in Holborn, The Army & Navy Stores in Victoria Street, and similar outlets in provincial towns. But the staging of the championships at Wimbledon in 1877 brought to sports goods suppliers and manufacturers the opportunity also to be the exclusive official supplier of balls to the body which organised the tournament, the All England Club.

ALL ENGLAND CLUB AND BALL SELECTION

The club's committee was not to be hurried into committing itself to a long-term arrangement for the supply of a ball that would best fit the

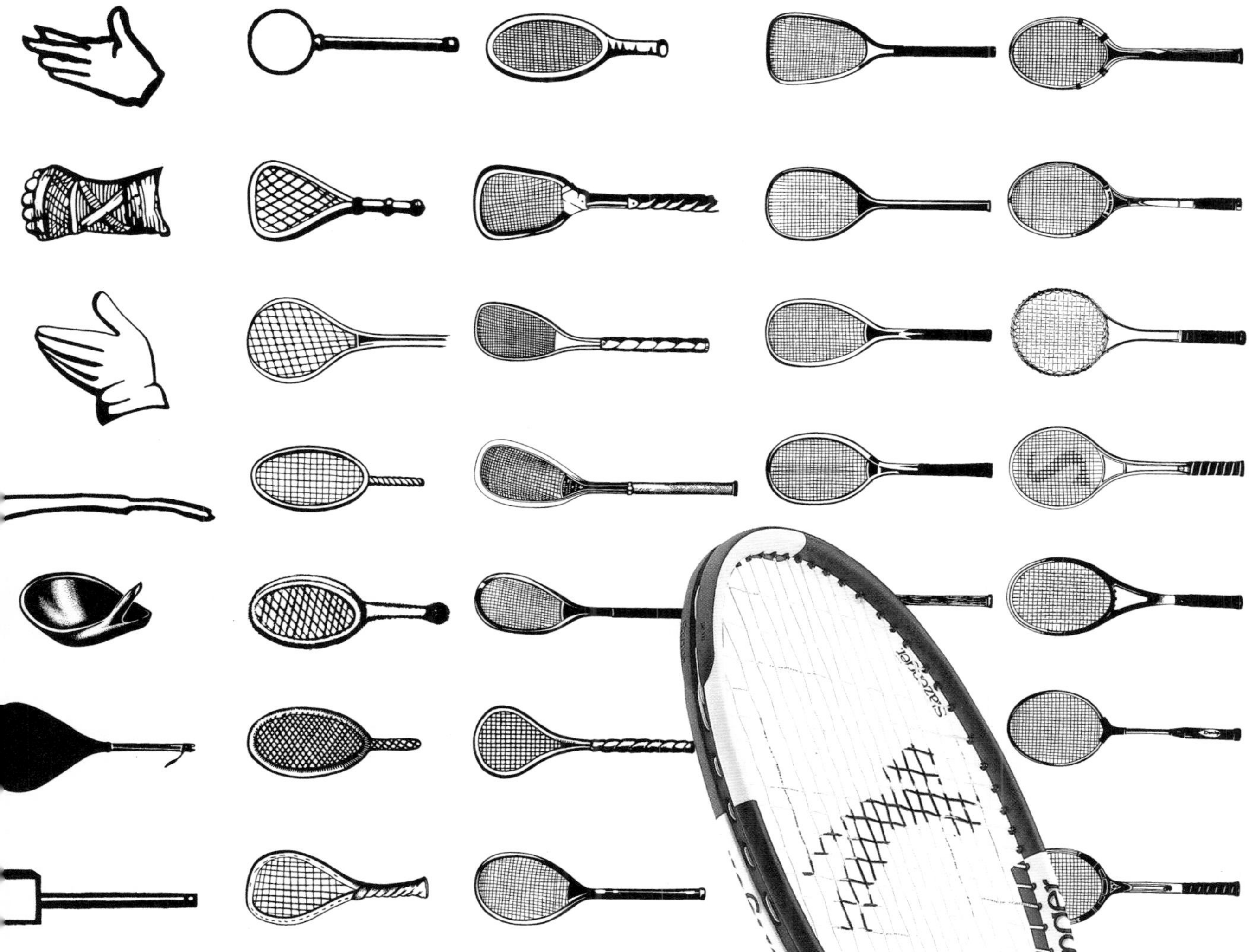

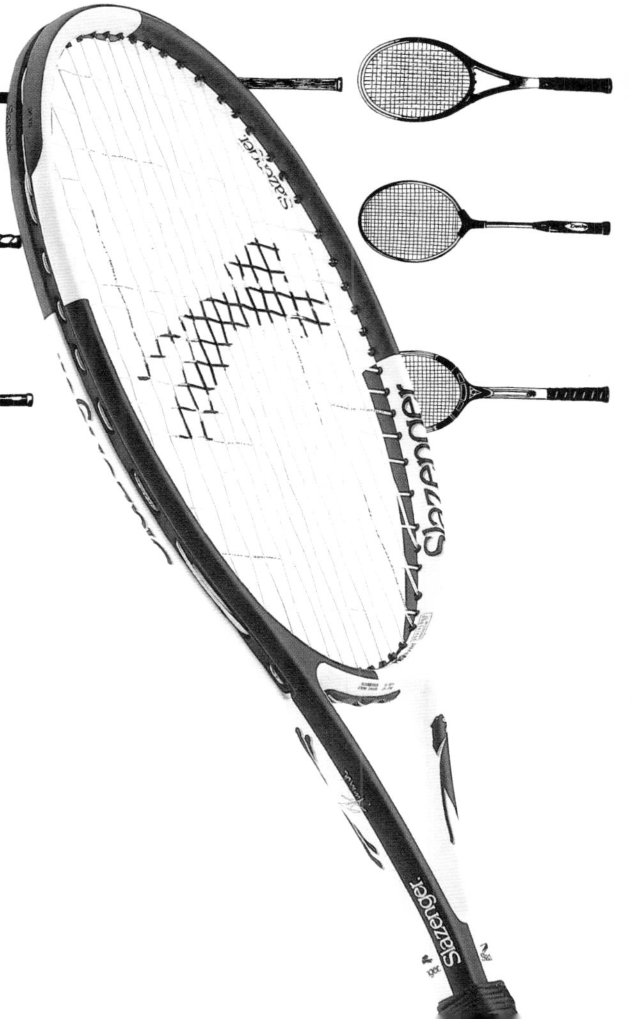

The general shape of the tennis racket, with its handle and bent wood elliptical frame, enclosing a network of cord or catgut, has changed little in 500 years. From using the hand to hit the balls it has evolved to today's Slazenger Pro Braided racket shown on the right.

17

THE NEW REGISTERED ROTARY LAWN TENNIS MARKER.

Large 16/6 each. Small 11/0 each.

RACKET PRESSES.

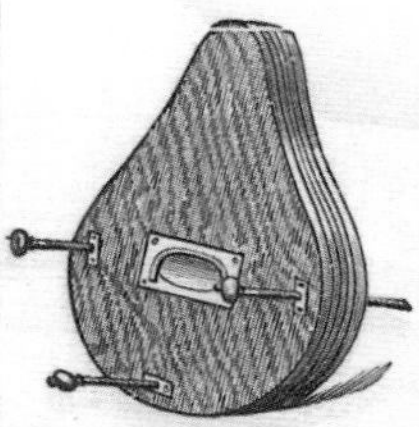

	PLAIN.		POLISHED.
BIRCH.—each.			
For 1 bat	3 2	...	3 8
2	3 9	...	4 3
4	5 6	...	6 6
6	7 0	...	8 0
MAHOGANY.—each.			
For 1	4 0	...	5 0
2	4 6	...	5 6
4	7 0	...	8 0
6	8 6	...	9 6

THE "CENTRAL" RACKET PRESS.

By Her Majesty's Royal Letters Patent.

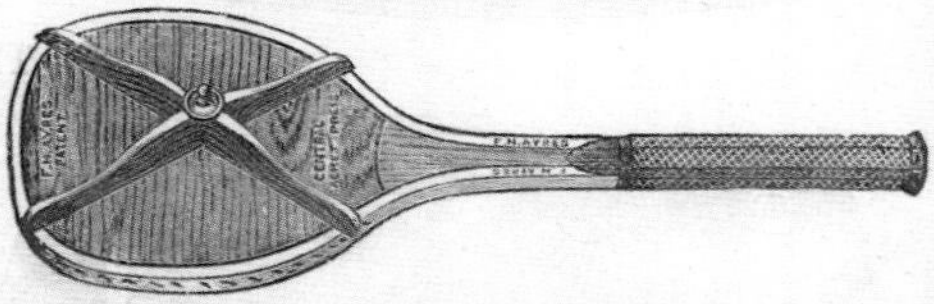

This new patent press is made to fit into the head of the racket on each side with polished walnut crosses and boards lined with green cloth. It is very handy, portable, and effective. Price 7/6 each.

THE "CENTRAL" RACKET PRESS.—Patent.

This handy press, consisting of a cross of wood placed on each side of the frame of the racket and connected by a screw through the gut, is the simplest and most perfect system of keeping a racket when not in use in its original shape. No player should be without one ; as it is well known the changes in the temperature affect the stringing of rackets. The central press, though

The "GRIP" RACKET PRESS,

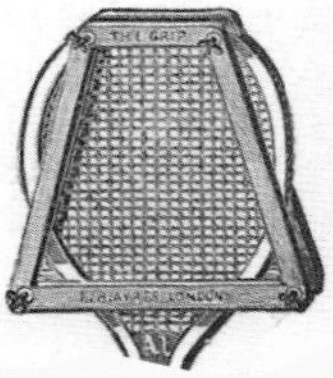

per doz.

SPECIAL SETS.

THE "REGISTERED GARDEN SEAT."

Regd. 5 and 6 Vic., Cap. 100.

MALTESE CROSS CROQUET.

From pages of F H Ayres's 1896 catalogue.

specification which they had drawn up with the greatest care. Their championship 'match' ball (as opposed to practice balls which were supplied by the gardener) had to have a flannel cover sewn by hand with unbleached heavy thread and with uncrossed stitches. Its weight could only vary from one and a quarter to one and a half ounces.

This flannel covering was introduced to lawn tennis by John Moyer Heathcote who, in 1875, had been the instigator of a commission to establish a new set of rules for the game which could be universally adopted. In the letter he wrote to *The Field* in 1874 he maintained that he had found advantage in covering balls with white flannel 'which made them bounce better, while they were also easier to see and control'. Compared with the uncovered India-rubber balls then generally used, the flannel cover provided air resistance which reduced their speed, stabilised their trajectory and made them heavier. Heathcote was an ardent player of Real Tennis, the balls for which were made with compressed rags with stitched flannel covers. Most of this flannel was made in the Leicestershire town of Melton Mowbray – a stout smooth cloth with the nap cut close and the face finished without pressing or glossing. This Melton cloth, which had served Real Tennis players, proved ideal for the lawn tennis game.

For that first tournament at Worple Road in 1877, the Club chose Jefferies and Company of Woolwich to supply fifteen dozen of the balls they had specified so carefully, and they were given the order again the following year. However, the balls for the 1879 tournament were supplied by F H Ayres who, more than sixty years later, were to become part of Slazenger.

Ayres were making a range of tennis balls from the uncovered rubber variety for play in the rain or on courts with rough surfaces to cemented and sewn covered balls and a new 'Terra-Cotta' brand adapted for asphalt courts. The one the All England Club chose for the 1879 championship was 'a superior, stout, rubber ball covered with fine melton cloth' (patent registration no 40979). Ayres named it 'The Wimbledon' and the public could buy it for 12 shillings a dozen. Those who took part in the Wimbledon championships played with balls supplied by Ayres for the next 22 years.

Neither the main business of J S Moss and Sons of Manchester, nor their Market Street branch, Slazenger et Fils, were in a position to supply the All England Croquet and Lawn Tennis Club with balls in 1877. They were busy building up their sports clothing and military tailoring business. However, once Slazenger et Fils were established in their larger Corporation Street premises, they steadily expanded their business into the many other facets of the sports trade in which the likes of Ayres, Sykes and Gradidge were firmly entrenched. In 1883 they felt confident enough to move out of Manchester and into the metropolis, the financial centre of the world and the meeting place for buyers from all over the British Empire. They acquired a factory in Holland Street, Woolwich, and offices on the Thames Embankment in the heart of the City of London at 56, Cannon Street in what was known as Laurence Pountney Hill.

The impact that the invention of Wingfield's Sphairistike/Lawn Tennis had on the sports trade was very considerable. No one could afford to do other than jump on the wagon, and hope to stay there. Ralph and Albert Slazenger engaged gear at once. They presented 'The New Game of Lawn Tennis' which Slazenger and Sons sold complete in a box. It was an immediate success. They were still India rubber goods manufacturers and waterproofers, legging and gaiter manufacturers, but also, as the trade directories of 1886 pointed out, 'cricket bat makers' and 'football and football boots manufacturers'. Moreover, their entry included the words 'lawn tennis rackets and appliances' – without indicating whether they were makers, or suppliers of gear made by others.

SLAZENGER 'DEMON' RACKET MADE ITS DEBUT IN THE 1880s

Their 'Demon' and 'Renshaw' tennis rackets were inscribed with the signature 'Slazenger and Sons' and sold for a guinea (£1 1s) and 12s 6d respectively. Their 'Guinea Demon' was 'guaranteed strung with 18-strand gut and perfect in every detail'. Every racket had a reference number and warranty. Later rackets bore names such as 'Lawford' and 'Ich Dien', which perhaps indicated it had been made for the Prince of Wales.

It was of course for players in the Wimbledon Championships to use whatever racket they liked, and, along with other suppliers, Slazengers made sure it was widely known whenever champions won the tournament with one of theirs. With the blessing, indeed encouragement, of the All England Club, suppliers used the championships to showcase their products, naming the specific racket with which the championship was won with the name of the winner. The Slazenger 'Renshaw' racket was named after William Renshaw who won the Wimbledon Championships six years on end, in 1881, 1882, 1883, 1884, 1885 and 1886, and then again in 1889. His twin brother Ernest won it in 1888. Separately and as doubles partners, the Renshaw twins won 13 titles between 1881 and 1889. The surge in the game's popularity was almost entirely on account of William and Ernest's spectacular performances, and was known as the Renshaw Smash. Indeed, in his history of the championships John Barrett, who joined Slazenger in 1955 and became a director in 1974, regards the two of them as creating the modern game, 'perfecting the smash, the hard service and aggressive volleying...'

Slazenger named several of their tennis rackets after tennis champions such as Renshaw and Lawford.

> William Renshaw transformed tennis from a pastime into a sport. Crowds came to watch the wealthy twins from Cheltenham, and special trains were run by the London and South Western Railway to a halt by the site of the All England Club. He was the founding father of tennis.

Slazenger did not start making tennis *balls* immediately they moved to London. In 1886 however the innovative Ralph Slazenger applied for a patent for an ingenious new game to be called Badminton Tennis. This involved a 'Tivey' (shuttlecock) being struck by 'tennis bats' over an elevated net with two movable courts, one each side of the net. The net should preferably, stated

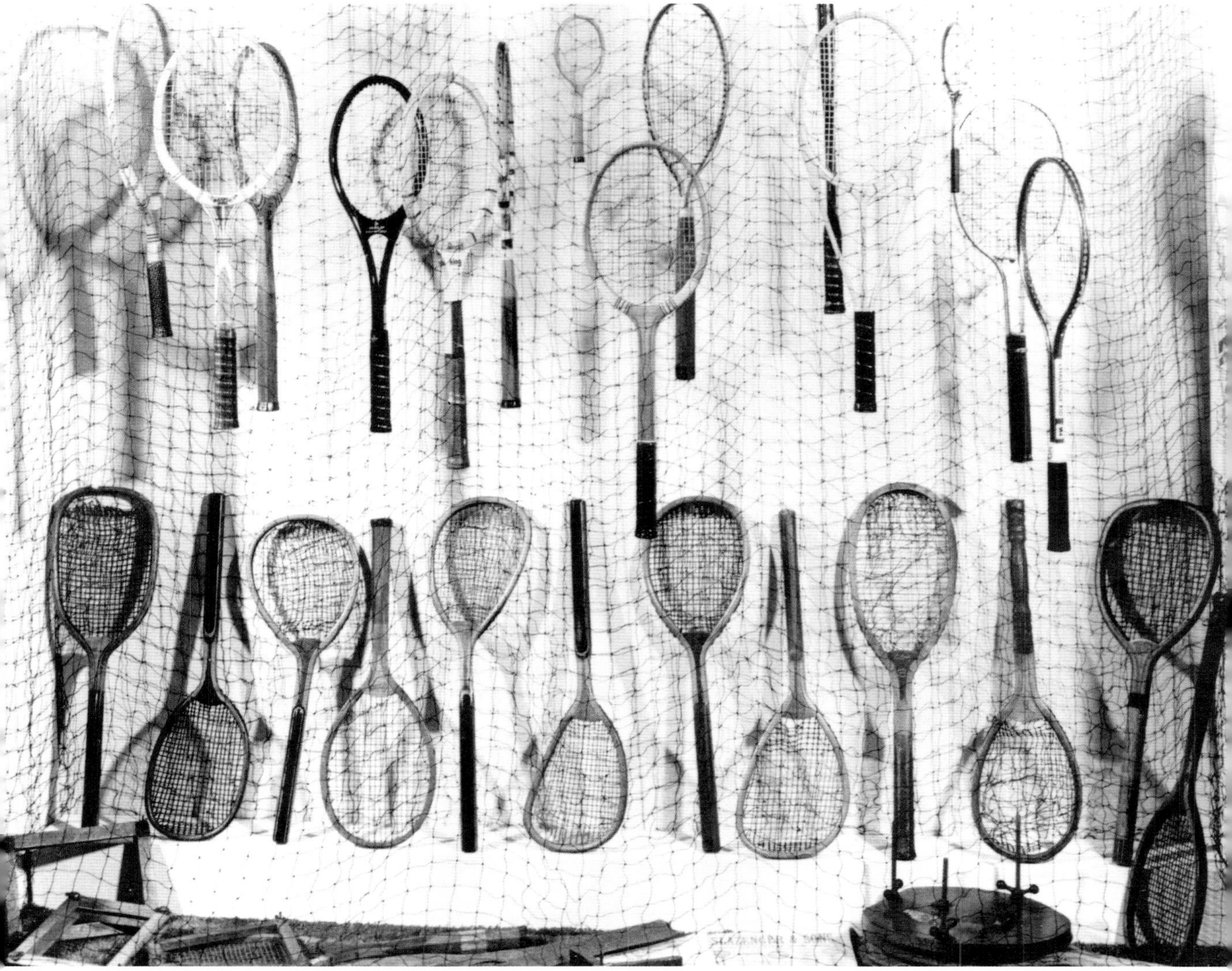

Part of Wimbledon's collection of rackets, old and new, used in the tournament.

the patent, be made of Japanese paper or any material that would emit a sound when struck by the tivey, 'so that the opponent would know whether or not it had landed in or out of his adversary's court'. Slazenger's Badminton Tennis never caught on. But in the following year, brother Albert, still calling himself Slazenger-Moss, applied for a patent for wool-covered tennis balls.

SLAZENGER REPLACED AYRES AS WIMBLEDON'S TENNIS BALL SUPPLIER

These first Slazenger tennis balls, made impervious to moisture 'by the introduction of a chemical preparation for the purpose of waterproofing woollen fabrics', were put into production at the company's Woolwich factory in 1887. There was

Date of Application, 11th Feb., 1887.
Specification Accepted, 1st Apr., 1887.

A.D. 1887, 11*th* FEBRUARY. N° 2173.

COMPLETE SPECIFICATION.

Improvements in Lawn Tennis and other Covered Balls.

I, ALBERT SLAZENGER-MOSS Manufacturer 56 Cannon Street London E.C. do hereby declare the nature of this invention and in what manner the same is to be performed, to be particularly described and ascertained in and by the following statement:—

My invention consists in applying to Lawn Tennis Balls, Woollen Covers impervious to moisture without altering the appearance, character of or the play of the Ball, by the introduction into the Woollen Covers of Lawn Tennis Balls a chemical preparation well known for the purpose of Waterproofing woollen fabrics by chemical process.

When this cover is cemented on to the Ball it is impervious to moisture and does not alter in weight when played in damp or wet places, and does not convey moisture to the racket in the same quantities as Ball covered with ordinary Woollen coverings does. For Waterproofing the cloth I use Castile Soap dissolved in water and alum dissolved in water, after passing the fabric several times through these solutions it becomes sufficiently waterproof when dried but I do not confine myself to this process of Waterproofing.

Having now particularly described and ascertained the nature of my said invention and in what manner the same is to be performed, I declare that what I claim is

The cloth covering of Lawn Tennis Balls with chemically Waterproofed covers.

Dated this eleventh day of February 1887.

ALBERT SLAZENGER-MOSS.

LONDON: Printed by DARLING AND SON.
For Her Majesty's Stationery Office.
1887.

[*Price 4d.*]

Price 25p

In 1887 Albert Slazenger invented a woollen cover made waterproof with a coating of Castile Soap before it was cemented on to rubber tennis balls.

no question, however, of Slazenger's immediately replacing F H Ayres as the exclusive suppliers of tennis balls to the Wimbledon Championships which by 1901, the year Queen Victoria died, they had been for 22 years. And not only for Wimbledon. Their 'Championship' ball, as they rightly stated in their advertising, had also been used in the principal tournaments throughout England, Ireland, Scotland, America and Australia 'and in all foreign countries where the game has any votaries'. They further claimed that 'the most flattering testimonials have been received from some of the most eminent players, all speaking as to the excellence of its qualities, as well in accuracy as in elasticity, reliability and finish'. By 1896, Ayres were able to offer ten different ball specifications to suit every pocket, all skill levels, all surfaces and weather conditions. Their patented 'Roughed' ball was not not only suited to asphalt courts but also, they said, 'highly satisfactory in the wet'.

It seemed unlikely that they would ever be dislodged from their position at Wimbledon. In 1902, however, the All England Lawn Tennis and Croquet Club appointed a new Secretary, Archdale Palmer. In the manner of new brooms, he marked the new regime under his administration with a sweeping change, one for which, he reckoned, he would have the support of those who took part in the championships. At the beginning of 1902 he was instrumental in arranging a round robin letter, signed by a number of senior players, which stated a preference for the Slazenger ball to be used in future championships. Although the club's committee had been satisfied with the Ayres ball, they responded to the players' pressure by agreeing to use Slazenger balls for the 1902 tournament, and for as long as the players wanted.

The All England 1902 switch to Slazenger balls was the single most important event in the company's history. It is unlikely that its full and lasting impact was apparent at the time, but the course of the Slazenger story would have been very different if Ayres had held on to the Wimbledon endorsement which they had first secured in 1879.

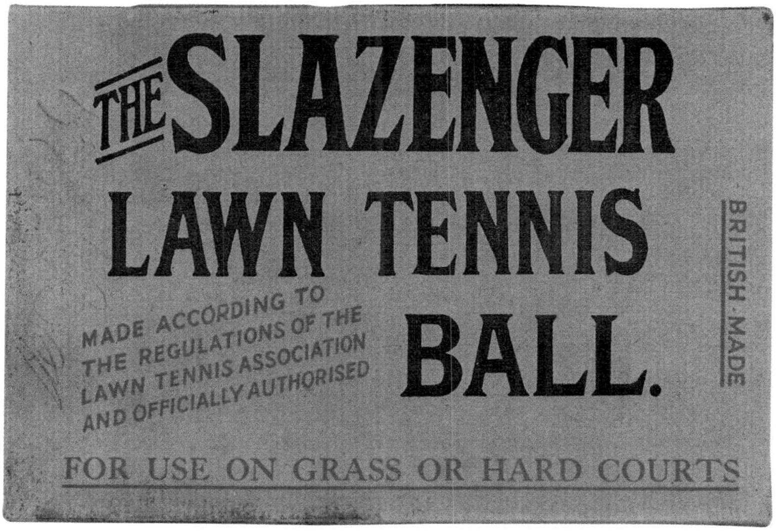

Packaging in the 1930s

ELLIMAN'S UNIVERSAL
EMBROCATION
Prepared by
ELLIMAN Sons & Co.
Slough
ENGLAND
IT
I WILL
HAVE OR
I WILL
HAVE
NONE
S.T. DADD
ELLIMAN'S
8½d
FOR
STIFFNESS. ACHES. SPRAINS. BRUISES.

2. Advantage Slazenger!

THE Wimbledon championships themselves changed in almost every respect in the 22 years when Ayres supplied the balls. Very many more balls were required than the 15 dozen provided for the amateur Gentlemen's Singles which comprised the first tournament of 1877. In 1884 they added a Ladies' Singles championship in which 13 took part. Women had begun playing tennis in the 1870s, dressed in heavy flannel or serge with maybe a bustle, which seriously constricted their movement. But anything else was not deemed suitably becoming. However, by the time 19-year-old Maud Watson, a vicar's daughter, became the first ladies' champion in 1884, they had changed their costumes to a lighter, white material, a colour which, as Ron Atkin has pointed out, 'helped to mask perspiration, the dreaded consequence of running'. In the same year the club added a Gentlemen's Doubles championship. Oxford University Lawn Tennis Club, which decided to stop holding the doubles tournament it had run since 1879, presented the trophy.

At the end of the nineteenth century, ladies who sported themselves on the tennis court made sure they were well covered – at first in heavy, brightly coloured serge with a bustle, and later in a lighter, white material – and never without a hat.

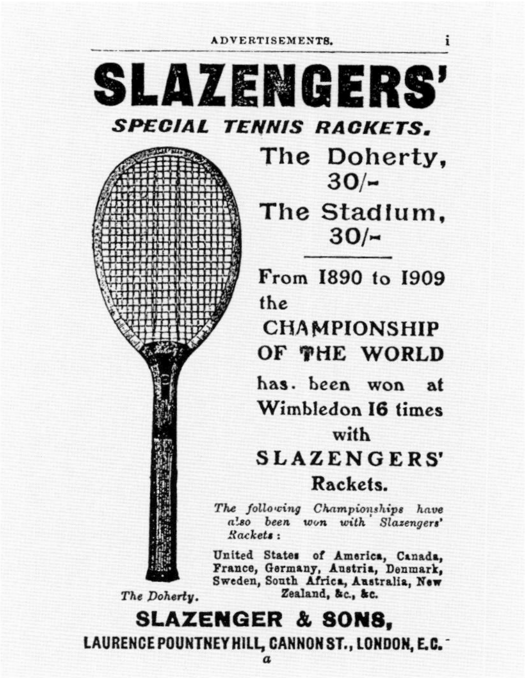

Wimbledon was known as the Championship of the World in 1910.

By the start of the twentieth century, the Wimbledon championships had become truly international. In 1905, the American May Sutton won the Ladies' Singles title, the first champion from overseas. Young men came from Australia and New Zealand to challenge the English and Irish champions. The few thousand who watched the amateur players battle it out from the seats around the centre court became used to French and German names such as Gobert, Decugis and Kleinschroth.

The game itself spread all over the world. The 'invincible and legendary' English couple Reginald and Laurence Doherty were the first great international tennis stars, winning nine singles and eight doubles titles between 1897 and 1906. Laurence was the first overseas player to win the United States Tennis Championships in 1903. The two brothers led the British team to victory four times in the new Davis Cup competition. They took the name of Slazenger with them.

In the course of the first decade of the new century, tennis players – would-be champions and those who played it for fun and exercise – had a choice of 23 Slazenger rackets, with the 'Doherty' frame heading the list. It cost £1 10s. 'The World's Championship,' declared the company, 'had been won no less than 15 times between 1890 and 1908 with our rackets, of which the highest honours in single-handed lawn tennis was secured with the "Doherty" racket for 11 consecutive years ending 1906, while both the World's Championship 1908, and the Covered Court Championships 1908, have been won with our new production, the "Slazenger"'.

The 'Demon' was still in great demand. Of it, *Land and Water* magazine said, 'For genuine good service we have not heard any racket better spoken of than this; it is a fine driver and stands wear well'. The All England club's endorsement of their tennis balls brought in vast orders for the product they named 'World's Championship Ball'. It had been selected for nine Wimbledon tournaments, five Dwight-Davis international competitions, and the 1904 and 1908 Olympics.

To build up overseas demand, they made rackets for Australasia named 'Colonial' and 'Kangaroo'; 'Cato' and 'Viceroy' for the Indian market 'and other tropical climates'. There were 'Colonial' tennis balls of many colours

Slazenger's 'Doherty' headed their list of 23 tennis rackets in 1910.

The choice for every Wimbledon Championship
since 1902
Slazenger Tennis Balls
The Doherty Brothers
John Beswick

SARTORIAL TENNIS.

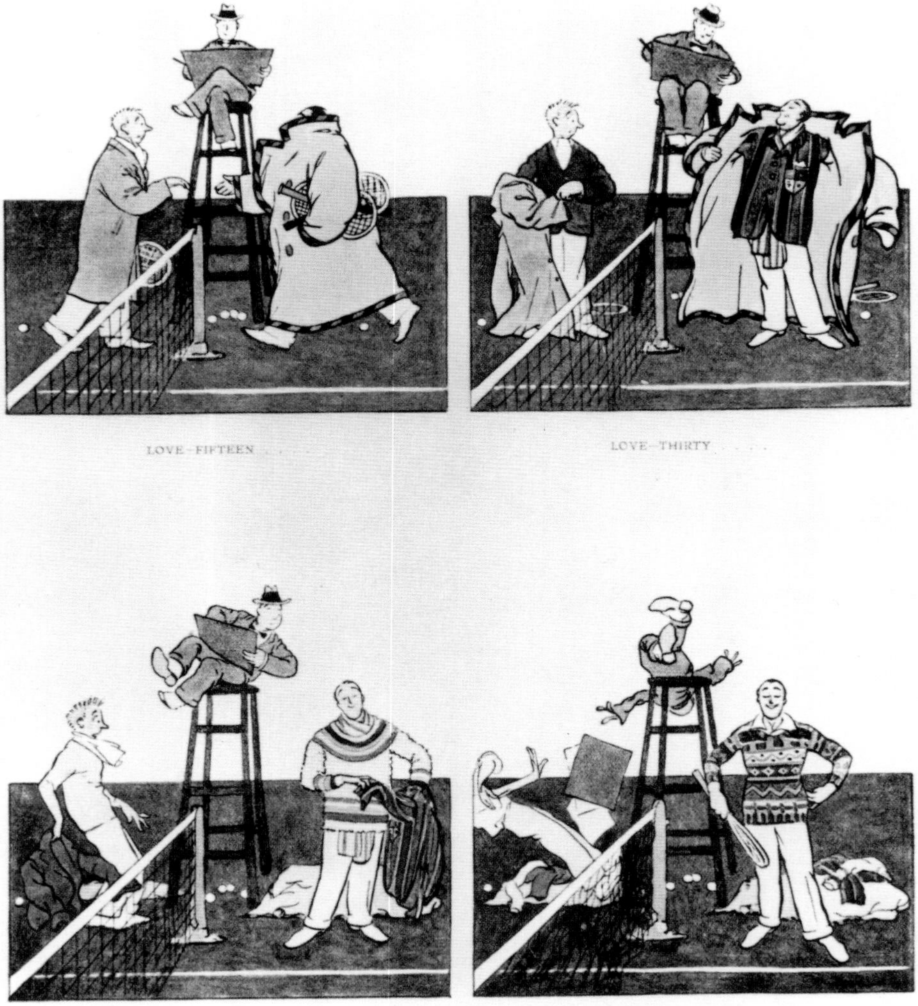

LOVE–FIFTEEN . . . .

LOVE–THIRTY . . . .

LOVE–FORTY

GAME.

They could never have done this in a bustle, but such high jinks were easy in Slazenger's liberated sports wear (bottom right).

Taken from the very first Slazenger ad in the Wimbledon programme.

designed for 'all countries situated at a great distance from where the ball is made, and where extremes of temperature have to be contended with'. They made their 'Tropical' tennis ball in 13 two-colour combinations, plus any other mix the customer wanted. It was deemed to be 'specially suited for hot climates or when the sun is very glaring'.

There had never been any let-up in catering for everything the tennis player needed, which was the basis of Slazenger's sports business. Alongside the rackets and balls, shoes and eyeshades, were all the items tournament organisers and the domestic player needed to equip the court on which all of it would be employed – the net, line tapes, stop netting, scorebooks and the rest, plus five complete boxed sets of tennis equipment.

The profit from these paled, however, beside that from tennis balls, the reputation and high sales of which derived in so large a way from their being used at the Wimbledon Championships. But their place as the Number One was not as secure as had been assumed. In 1905 their status as championship ball supplier was queried by one of the Wimbledon referees on the grounds that the balls were the 'wrong' size and therefore illegal. He felt so strongly about it that he resigned. Naturally enough, the All England club committee was reluctant to lose the benefit of having the balls supplied free of charge, and rejected the referee's call to substitute another make for Slazenger's.

Unfortunately for Slazenger, the referee in question was also a journalist, and let it be known that the firm had made it a practice to send the club an annual gift of £100; not only that, but was also contributing to the cost of the Lawn

The "FIELD" says.—"Messrs. Slazenger & Sons have sent us a gut which stands a comparatively enormous strain. A 'Demon' Racket so strung has more drive than any we have yet tried or seen tried."
THE
DEMON
LAWN TENNIS
RACKET
TRADE MARK
THE
DEMON
REGD
"This device on every genuine Demon"
Slazenger
Every Racket bears the "DEMON" Stamp.
BEWARE OF IMITATIONS.
Sole Makers SLAZENGER & SONS LONDON.

Tennis Association's *Journal*. It was a good 'story' for the press, and no newspaper or periodical editor could afford to neglect it. All kinds of other suggestions were made about Slazenger's behaviour, and some of the press comment hinted that maybe Archdale Palmer, the club's secretary, had too much influence in such matters.

Although Slazenger came in for a great deal of criticism at this time, mainly because it was felt in some quarters that they had too strong a hold on the game, particularly in relation to supplying balls to the major tournaments at no charge, they had not been alone in pursuing the endorsement policy. Ayres had operated similar arrangements for the Bournemouth and Eastbourne tournaments. The All England club came through it all unscathed, but Archdale Palmer resigned.

A few months later, the directors of Slazenger and Sons Ltd offered him a place on their board, which he accepted. They then appointed him managing director. The next year, 1906, the All England club decided that in future they would pay the makers of the selected official championship ball for all those used in the fortnight's tournament.

FOUNDER RALPH SLAZENGER DIES

Lawn tennis had been firmly established as Slazenger's main field of operation. The number of titles won with Slazenger rackets, together with the ball adoption, was central to the promotional thrust of the business. In their 1910 catalogue, covering all aspects of their sports trade, they emphasised this marketing priority by highlighting the company's four main tennis rackets: 'Demon', 'Doherty', 'Slazenger' and 'E.G.M', which was 'made from the instructions of the well-known expert Mr E G Meers, to whose recognised mechanical knowledge we are indebted for the production of this magnificent racket'. They did not place their 'Gore' racket, made to the instructions of Mr A W Gore, All England Champion in 1902 and 1908, in the top four, in spite of it being one of the five Slazenger frames, out of the range of 30, with the highest price of £1 10s.

The price/volume relationship was a key factor with the 'Demon', to which, in the catalogue, Slazenger gave the most dramatic presentation. At 15 shillings, it was half the price of the 'Gore' in 'Ordinary' quality, although 21

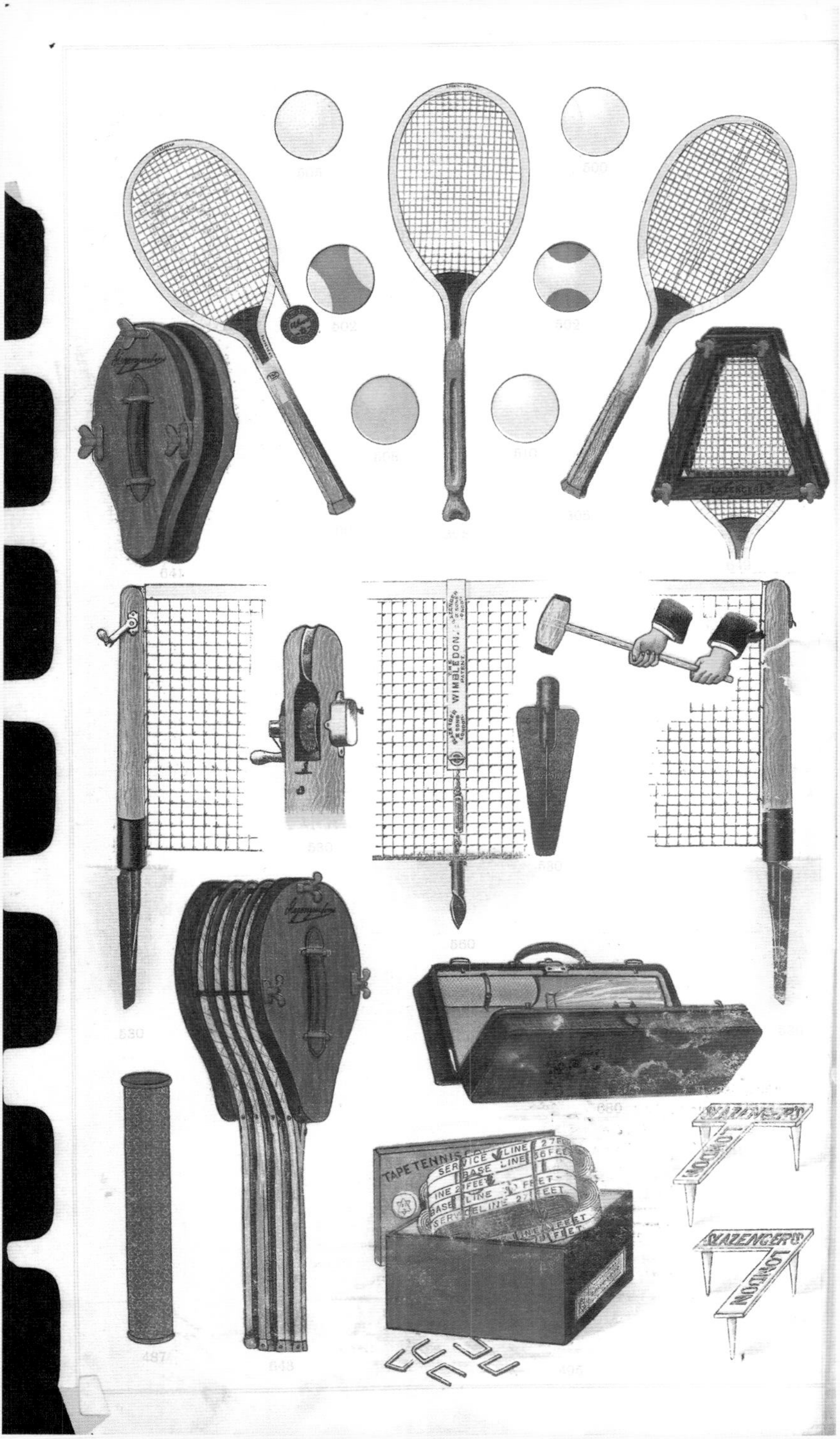

In 1910, as their catalogue shows, Slazenger were selling more than tennis balls and rackets.

Ralph Slazenger, who died in 1910.

shillings in the 'Special' version. The 'Demon' was described as having the largest sale of any Slazenger racket. Would-be buyers were warned that this had induced 'unprincipled dealers to introduce spurious imitations'. They therefore begged to caution the public to see that 'The Demon' was stamped on every racket.

In this same year of 1910, Ralph Slazenger died, his name, as obituaries all over the world observed, 'a familiar one wherever lawn tennis is played'.

They recalled, too, how for 30 years he had served as a volunteer in the Lancashire Light Infantry from which he retired with the rank of captain; and how, as Master of the Needlemakers Company and a member of seven other livery companies, he had devoted a great deal of his time to the activities of the City of London Corporation. In 1909 he was elected a Sheriff. He engaged in much charitable work – as a Governor of the Royal National Orthopaedic Hospital, Christ's Hospital and the Royal School for Deaf Children.

Although by now Archdale Palmer had become a major influence in the conduct of the family firm, Ralph's early death at the age of 64 was a huge blow.

ALBERT LED COMPANY INTO DOMINANT POSITION IN TENNIS MARKET

His younger brother Albert became sole owner. Like Ralph, he was a prominent member of Society. As well as involving himself in Corporation of London affairs in the Gold and Silver Wyre Drawer's Company, he had succeeded his brother on the City's Court of Common Council for the Dowgate Ward in which Laurence Pountney Hill was located. He took over as chairman of the company which he had founded with Ralph 29 years earlier. Only the year before, he had married Leila Gully, a keen golfer who had been captain of the Ladies' Parliamentary Golfing Association, an excellent tennis player and had narrowly missed international honours at hockey. She was fully qualified to support the husband who, within 12 months of their marriage, found himself with the responsibility, together with the able Archdale Palmer, for keeping Slazenger's place of eminence in the sports trade.

The financial base he inherited was substantial. He at once turned the business into a public limited company titled Slazenger's Ltd. The share capital structure was 100,000 £1 cumulative preference shares and 165,000 £1 ordinary shares. As vendor, Albert took one third of each class of shares as part payment of the purchase consideration. The flotation was presented against the background of a profits record over the previous ten years showing a rise from £26,787 in 1901 to £38,836 in 1910. At the first shareholders' meeting in April 1912, Albert announced that the profit for the year ending December had again risen, to £41,882. He declared a ten per cent dividend on the ordinary shares, and increased the general reserve fund to £15,413.

The trade journal *Sports Trader* commented that it appeared that the business of the company had been well maintained in all departments, 'the demand showing an increase both with regard to the home and export trade'. The basis of this success was the company's increasingly dominant position in a tennis market that was benefiting from the game's ever-widening popularity.

Regrettably, the criticism of the All England club's relationships with Slazenger, which had been made by that referee/journalist in 1905, re-surfaced in 1913. At that year's annual meeting of the Lawn Tennis Association, a Mr P W Rootham announced that 'representations had been made to the committee of the All England Club that the method employed by them of selecting the ball for the championships was bad, but they had practically been ignored'. Rootham went on to suggest that, while the club had stated their selection method was based on asking the players to choose the ball, he had grave doubts whether the ball was in fact selected in this way. He further alleged that 'a portion' of the committee saw to it that one particular ball was chosen year after year; that a ring had been formed for this purpose and thus a monopoly created. He went on to name two committee members. One of them was the father of Laurence Doherty, winner of five Men's Singles titles. Doherty owned Slazenger shares, and therefore stood to benefit, in the form of dividends, from trading results that would be favourably affected by the ball connection with the championships.

The club committee took this allegation sufficiently seriously to place it before an eminent barrister. After a formal enquiry, counsel reported to the Lawn Tennis Association and All England club that, while he felt it was wrong in principle for a committee member to be involved in a voting procedure that could be regarded as having a benefit for a company in which he is interested, he was satisfied that 'neither of them had any improper motive in taking part in a vote or were influenced in any way by their holdings of shares in the commercial company owning the ball selected'. He was also satisfied that 'the votes given by the two members in question in no way affected the result arrived at'.

For some reason Rootham thought better of actually attending the enquiry himself. None of those who did attend, and were questioned by learned counsel, had any complaint to make about the selection method.

SLAZENGER'S 'WORLD CHAMPIONSHIP' BALL IS THEIR BEST SELLER

As mentioned earlier, the specification of the 'official' ball for the first Wimbledon championship tournament in 1877 was drawn up by the All England Club which had taken over the management of the game from the Marylebone Cricket Club; and then in 1888 handed it over to Britain's newly formed Lawn Tennis Association, one of several round the world – seven years after a United States National Lawn Tennis Association, adopting the All England rules, had been formed in 1881. When 13 national lawn tennis associations met in Paris in March 1913 and formed the International Lawn Tennis

continued on page 30

Preparing tennis ball covers for vulcanizing at the Woolwich factory in the 1920s.

The evolution of the tennis ball, and the way it was manufactured, was transformed by Major Wingfield's invention of lawn tennis in 1874. For many hundreds of years previously the balls for the earlier forms of the game, in particular real tennis, had generally been covered with leather and filled with various materials including feathers and sand, wool and cotton and, frequently, with hair – in *Much Ado About Nothing* Shakespeare tells us that the full

A box of balls in 1928 – each ball individually wrapped.

growth of Benedick's beard had often served the purpose of filling tennis balls.

Charles Goodyear's early-19th-century invention of the vulcanisation process for rubber led to the introduction of hollow balls, which were extremely bouncy. The early lawn tennis enthusiasts, who found these balls difficult to handle on firm courts, used a red hot knitting needle to make holes in the balls to produce a lower bounce.

Heathcote's 1874 experiment with flannel covers resulted in the forerunner of the modern ball, which was available for the first Wimbledon championships in 1877. The Ayres' balls, probably imported from Germany, which were used at the tournament from 1879 to 1901, and at the first US Open in 1881, featured the steadily improving Melton cloth covers by then being specially produced for tennis balls. These covers were used on the Slazenger balls first used at Wimbledon in 1902, and which were hand sewn with no two alike.

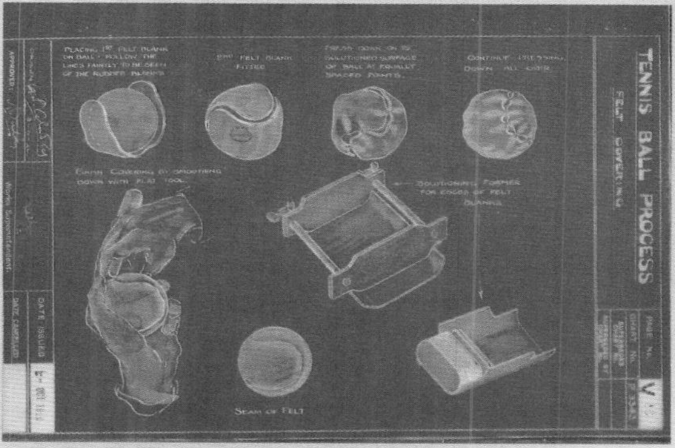

Page from a 1920s manual of tennis ball production.

It was not until 1914 that the Lawn Tennis Association took the first steps to define the features required for a tennis ball and to draw up a specification that would provide a uniform product. Even today it is possible to have balls with different playing characteristics determined by the rubber compound in the core and by the type of covering cloth, but an internationally observed specification defines the size, weight,

Applying the covers to the cores.

Removing tennis balls from a moulding machine.

hardness and rebound height of the officially approved balls. It also requires that the ball surface must be smooth and free from stitching.

From the 1920s increasingly sophisticated vulcanizing processes were used to produce the cores and also to 'weld' the outer cover to the core. Continual research by the leading ball manufacturers, working closely with the tennis governing bodies, has steadily improved the playing performance of the balls and has also led to the modernisation of the manufacturing process, much of which has been converted to robotisation.

Slazenger, with 115 years of manufacturing experience and its Research and Development team based at their main factories, first at Woolwich and later in Yorkshire, has always been at the forefront of tennis ball development. Their 'Hydroguard' moisture repellant ball, launched at the 2002 championships, is only the latest in a long line of significant product improvements pioneered by the company since 1887 and this work will continue to provide even better balls in the future both for the leading professionals and the recreational player.

Core covering at Horbury in the 1960s – still by hand.

Preparing the cover cloth before cutting into dumb-bells.

The centenary pack for the new Hydroguard moisture-repellant ball.

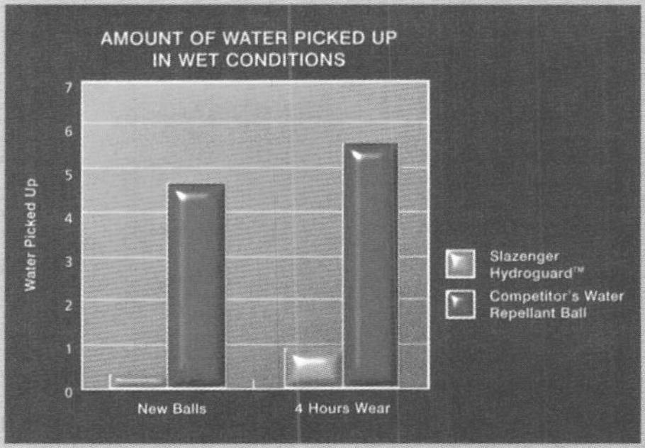

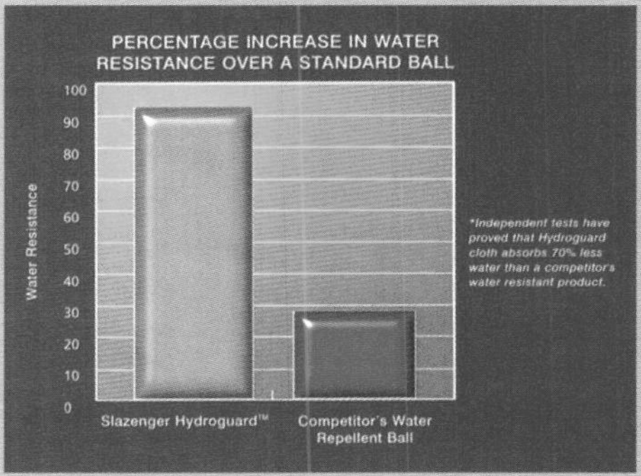

'On the ball'... ten facts about the tennis ball...

- Very early balls were hand made of leather
- As long ago as 1887 Slazenger patented waterproofing for tennis balls
- Coloured tennis balls (including two tone varieties) were used in non-Championship matches in the early 20th Century
- Balls were originally filled with compressed air to provide their bounce, today environmentally safe gases are used
- In the 1950s, balls made of rubber with no cloth covering were produced for use on hard courts

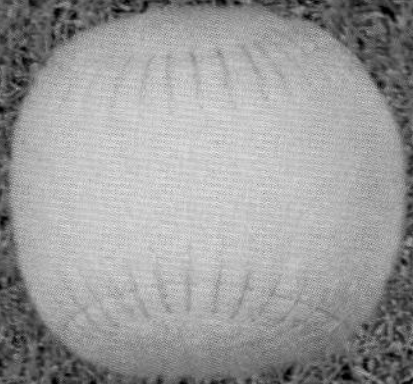

1902 *Slazenger's first year at The Championships. Each ball was hand sewn and no two were exactly alike. Construction by this time was of rubber with a wool cloth covering, a development of the original leather ball.*

1909 *Now the ball is made by understitching the covering. This same ball type had been used not only at Wimbledon but also at the British Olympic Games in London in 1908.*

1922 *The ball was understitched and still made by hand through a lengthy and highly skilled process.*

1950 *Consistency was now reaching new levels thanks to improving production technology. Now even the thickness of the core walls became standardised.*

1954 *'Nylon-Armour' was introduced. This was a coating on the covering to further improve wear and prolong playing characteristics.*

1965 *'Nylon-Armoured' balls were still current technology. Their 'rough frictional surface' was made to last longer for improved ball control.*

1967 *Around this time, player feedback led to the balls becoming slightly firmer and more durable.*

1982 *Fluorescent yellow balls are developed, rejecting the earlier green approach.*

1986 *Yellow balls are used at The Championships for the first time to make visibility easier for players, spectators and the TV audience.*

1997 *Hi Vis balls are developed. These are 10% brighter than standard tennis balls and are designed to increase visibility even further.*

2000 *Ultra Vis balls an improvement on Hi Vis are introduced for official use at The Championships for the first time.*

- To qualify for use at the Championships today each ball must have a bounce of more than 134.62cms and no less than 147.32cms when dropped from a height of 254cms onto a rigid surface
- Each ball must weigh between 56.7g and 58.7g
- When in play, the ball must have a deformation of less than 5.97mm
- At the 2002 Championship at Wimbledon some 36,000 balls will be used in all the various matches played, each and every ball used must comply with the rigorous standards laid down

1929 *Balls were made using a vulcanizing process and by cementing the cloth onto the 'core.'*

1937 *On Centre Court, a special refrigerator maintained the correct temperature (68 degrees) of the tournament balls.*

1939 *Patented 'K' cloth was used for the first time as a covering. This meant better wear and endurance characteristics for the ball.*

1946 *Play commences at The Championships after the Second World War with ball technology unchanged.*

1972 *Production processes were further improved to reduce distortion during play.*

1976 *For this season balls were available in white and yellow. White was retained for use at The Championships.*

1977 *As an attempt at achieving higher levels of visibility, green balls were introduced but were never officially adopted for The Championships.*

1981 *To celebrate their centenary year Slazenger produced a special ball. The core was made from the highest quality natural rubber and the covering of a wool and nylon mix. Now a sought after classic!*

2002 *This year, for the first time, a new Slazenger Wimbledon Ultra Vis ball will be used. The ball is treated with a water repellent barrier called 'Hydroguard™.' This results in less weight gain for the ball and more consistent performance over a longer time. To celebrate 100 years at Wimbledon Slazenger has produced a specially imaged 1902-2002 ball which is sure to become highly collectable.*

THE CHAMPIONSHIPS WIMBLEDON

Slazenger
OFFICIAL BALL TO WIMBLEDON 1902-2002

continued from page 23

Federation as the game's supreme governing body responsible for its laws (including the specification of the 'legal' ball) all of them joined, except the United States LTA. Not only was the USA the first nation to form such an association but in 1900 one of their leading players, Dwight Davis, founded the international competition – the Davis Cup. In 1913 they boycotted the new Federation and took exception to the Wimbledon tournament calling itself the World Championships.

Slazenger saw no reason to change the name of their best-selling tennis ball, the 'World Championship', though maybe brother Frank, who was the company's representative in America, was subjected to a certain amount of sarcastic ribaldry from those from whom he expected to receive orders.

A more serious setback to sales was the outbreak, two months after the 1914 Wimbledon tennis championships ended, of hostilities, by Britain and her Allies, against the Kaiser's Germany which became the First World War that was to last four years.

The life which was soon nostalgically remembered as Before The War was suspended, including the Wimbledon fortnight, while the nation organised itself for the single purpose of winning the war. More than ten per cent of Slazenger's staff, some 125, joined up in the armed forces to help their country achieve its aim; 15 of them were killed in active service. Production at Woolwich was severely cut due to wartime restrictions. Supplies to customers were limited, though the company continued to offer most of its pre-war range. If Wimbledon was on hold 'for the duration', people manning the Home Front continued to enjoy playing tennis on their garden lawns at home, at tennis clubs, on the many public courts, at school and college, as they had always done, but now relied on, also, for relief from the stress and strain of wartime.

The hatred of the enemy manifested itself in the pillorying of shops and restaurants, performers and manufacturers with German-sounding names who, it was taken for granted, were German nationals. Why should anyone in Britain, of the race whom Britain were fighting, be allowed to trade and profit here? Tennis racket gut manufacturer C Gibbs & Co of Nottingham told their customers that, as it was more than probable that Slazenger was a German firm, they should be closed down. When Slazenger's solicitors requested withdrawal of this damaging allegation, Gibbs's reply was less than placatory. 'Will you please say,' they answered, 'whether there is any just reason why your firm should not be closed down as an alien enemy, and why publicity should not be given?' Following further exchanges, Gibbs, while beginning to sound rather less sure of their case, still demanded, 'If not German, will you please say what nationality Slazenger is?'

The high quality of Slazenger's 'Doherty', and the other tennis rackets which they marketed, derived from the traditional expertise of the craftsmen at their Woolwich factory, seen here in the frame finishing room.

At work in the Woolwich factory vulcanizing the stitchless and seamless 'Slazenger' tennis balls selected for 1928 Wimbledon.

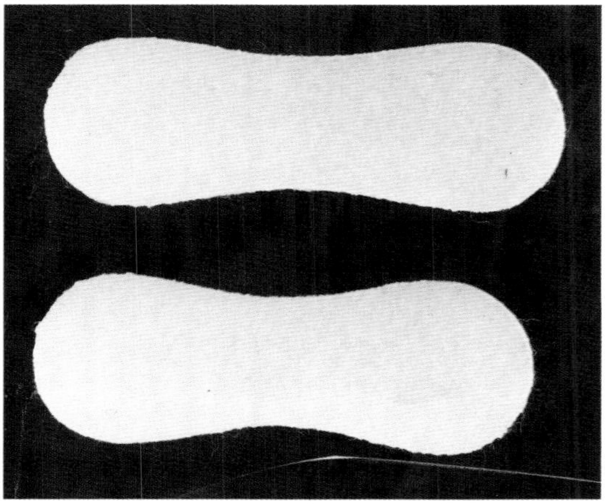

The rubber core of a tennis ball is covered by two Melton cloth figure-of-eight 'dumb-bells' like this.

So Slazenger turned to the High Court asking for a perpetual injunction to restrain Gibbs from making any further statements of this sort. They persuaded a former Lord Mayor of London and a director of Gamages to tell the court the damage such an allegation, if repeated, would make. When Archdale Palmer came into the witness box to speak on behalf of the company of which he was managing director, Mr Justice Astbury declared, 'If it will help this case any, I can vouch for the fact that Captain Palmer is not a German.' He had in fact been fighting the Germans as an infantry officer in the Essex Regiment, and been invalided out. Palmer told the court that all the directors of Slazenger were British born subjects, and that only one of their employees was a foreigner and he was Swiss. 'To call a person or a firm German at the present time,' said the judge, 'is as defamatory a statement as could possibly be made' – and promptly granted Slazenger their requested injunction against Gibbs, with costs.

The case was widely reported. In its editorial, *Sports Trader* welcomed its outcome and emphasised the outstanding merits of Slazenger as one of a number of manufacturers to have established the supremacy of British sporting goods.

> When we think of the hundreds of thousands of tennis rackets that are made and sold not only in this country but also in America and all other countries where the game of tennis is known and played, it is a great thing for any one firm to be able to claim that they are the makers of a racket that has had a larger sale than any other racket on the market, either in this country or abroad. The firm that holds that proud position is Messrs Slazenger Ltd. And the racket is their world famous 'Demon'.

FOUR YEARS OF WAR CRIPPLED SPORTS TRADE, RAISED PRICES

After four years of war, the sports trade had shrunk to a derisory size compared with the boom years that ended with that Wimbledon tournament of 1914. Those that delighted in tennis, ran a *Daily Express* report, 'have about as much chance of buying a dozen great auk's eggs as of obtaining a dozen tennis balls'. The paper quoted a representative of Slazenger as saying that even with a quarter of the normal number of workpeople, 'we engage only a small percentage in making tennis balls, as there are Government inspectors to see that a major part of the work is of national importance. Men who would ordinarily make tennis balls are covering electric wires with rubber which means our customers are strictly rationed'.

The pressure on production costs was very considerable. A circular issued in June 1918 advised an immediate ten per cent increase in the price of tennis balls. A warning on the front of the price list stated that 'as the prices named herein are all liable to revision without notice, orders can only be accepted at prices ruling at time of delivery'. However, the results for 1918

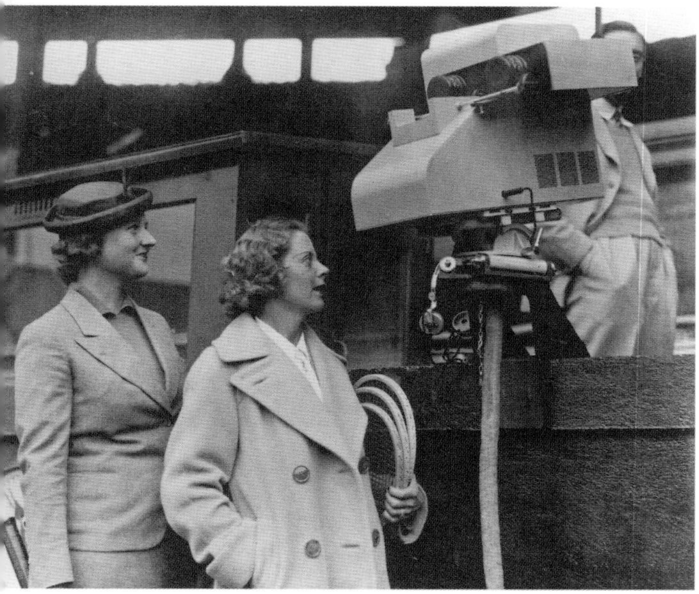

Two lady competitors suitably impressed by the first TV camera on the Centre Court in 1937.

showed a record profit of £57,400. There was larger turnover in every branch, but the returns from the activity with which the Slazenger family began their business, waterproofing, were particularly good. Rubber was used not only for insulating electric wire, but making a large range of bags and holdalls made, as their catalogue pointed out, 'in strong waterproof canvas'.

When the victorious Allies declared an armistice on November 11, 1918, and the following year signed a peace treaty, demobbed technicians and managers returned from the battlefields to resume their peacetime occupations and to see that Britain recovered her industrial eminence as swiftly as her exhausted state would allow. The sports trade picked up at a remarkable speed, owing mainly to the rapid growth of interest in sport of every kind, and lawn tennis in particular – playing it, watching it, reading about it.

The game became enormously popular, as Robert Graves pointed out, not only among the well-to-do, who had held a prejudice against it as a less manly game than cricket, but among the middle classes who had not hitherto had any facilities for playing.

> Its social advantages were obvious. Now that women had added thirty points to their game by rationalizing their dress and adopting the over-arm service, mixed doubles were no longer a nuisance to be gallantly borne, but a real pleasure. And in half an hour's tennis one could get quicker and better exercise than in three hours of club cricket. Wimbledon tennis was attended by thousands instead of hundreds, new clubs sprang up everywhere, local authorities provided public courts in parks.
>
> Robert Graves and Alan Hodge, *The Long Weekend*, Hutchinson 1940

TENNIS BECOMES MORE POPULAR THAN EVER WITH THE PEACE

More than any other to boost the interest in tennis was the French player with the bandeau, Suzanne Lenglen, who had won her first world championship on hard courts in Paris two months before the outbreak of the Great War. She was only 20 when she turned up at Wimbledon for the first post-war tournament of 1919 and defeated Dorothea Chambers who was ladies' champion in 1903 and 1904, 1906, 1910 and 1911, 1913 and the last pre-war event in 1914. Ten thousand watched Lenglen beat Chambers in that 1919 final of the ladies' singles.

'And for 20 times that number,' wrote John Collier in *Just The Other Day*, 'a new enthusiasm had come into being.'

Tennis was already news, but Mlle Lenglen made it, for a full fortnight of every year, the most important news of the day. There had been a victory march of London troops on the morning of that final, and the King and Queen, having watched that valedictory parade pass Buckingham Palace, had motored to Wimbledon to witness the arrival of an archetypal figure of the Peace... Until Suzanne arrived Mrs Lambert Chambers had not been defeated at Wimbledon for 11 years, and been seven times woman's champion – and it did not matter, for only

The tweed suits, the homburg hats, the caps – and the price of entrance – dates this queue for Wimbledon tickets as between-the-Wars.

Setting the stage for Wimbledon Fortnight, involving energetic hand-power and horse-power (note the boots to protect the surface), was more labour-intensive in the 1920s.

> tennis enthusiasts knew her by sight, and only her friends knew her Christian name; but everyone knew Suzanne.

The Suzanne Lenglen Cult was only the first stage in the 1920s transformation of the game of lawn tennis into the popular sport it had never been Before The War. Nineteen twenty saw the arrival of another phenomenon, the American Bill Tilden, whom many regard as the greatest player in the history of the game. In 1920 the Wimbledon championships were held for the first time on the much larger Church Road site and two years later the demand for centre court seats was so great that the club introduced the ballot system. On this surge in the popularity of the game Slazenger rode high, intensified by the enthusiasm and drive of a new recruit Edward (Tim) Hadingham who, in 1921, within three years of his joining the team at Laurence Pountney Hill, was taken on to the board. It was the year the company had a stand of revolutionary design at the British Industries Fair. A central feature of it was a showcase displaying Slazenger products 'which had added laurels to the reputation of the firm'.

Among them was a 'Doherty' racket with which visitors were told 'championships had been won 17 times', and a tennis ball used at Wimbledon and at the Olympics.

SLAZENGER WON THE TENNIS BALL WAR

Slazenger's relationship with Wimbledon came under scrutiny once again, in 1927, on the outbreak of the 'Tennis Ball War' between the Lawn Tennis Association and the tennis ball manufacturers.

The LTA had long held the view that the price of balls to the public was too high. Without consulting the firms that made them, they circulated a tender for an 'Official Ball'. This was accompanied by an agreement to be signed by the successful supplier, which required that the ball should be distributed without indicating who made it. Under the agreement the supplier was committed to charge buyers its maximum price of 15s 6d a dozen, which compared with a general price for premium balls in the range of 18s 6d to 19s 6d a dozen.

The majority of manufacturers objected very strongly to what they regarded as an attempt to impose drastic restrictions on the tennis ball business. However, retailers, who had for some time been unhappy with the way manufacturers supplied balls direct to clubs and tournaments at favourable prices, expressed interest in the LTA scheme, although they had reservations about the likely impact on their margins if the 15s 6d price for the LTA approved ball became the norm for all premium products.

In the event, only one manufacturer, John Jacques & Son Ltd, submitted a tender to the LTA, and they were duly appointed to supply the authorised ball. This prompted speculation as to whether the 'official ball' would be adopted for the 1928 Wimbledon championships instead of the Slazenger ball. The new Jacques ball was indeed used at a number of the main LTA events that year, but the Wimbledon authorities were quick to point out that their selection was made by the joint committee of management of the championships consisting of 12 members of the All England club and four representatives of the LTA council.

While the LTA representatives could not do other than recommend the Jacques ball, the secretary and manager of the All England club, Major D R Larcombe, announced that the Slazenger stitchless and seamless ball had been chosen on the basis of a series of playing tests carried out with unmarked balls. It was reported at the time that these tests had been instituted to 'ensure that overseas competitors [players] should have no grounds for complaint that they were called upon to use in the championships a ball which was disappointing to them'. The Slazenger connection with Wimbledon was maintained, although the LTA initiative certainly affected the company's future ball pricing and marketing policy.

In the month before the start of the 1928 Wimbledon, the company brought out what they called 'Two Best Sellers'. These were a 'Slazenger' stitchless and seamless ball which they presented as being exclusively selected for the 1928 tournament, priced at 19s 6d a dozen; and a brand new 'Demon' ball at 16s a dozen, advertised as 'a lower priced ball having all the characteristics of the best model', and 'unquestionably the world's finest value'.

Whether or not the LTA felt that their Official Ball project had had the desired effect and was therefore fully justified, by making the tennis ball industry introduce good quality balls at a lower price, is not known. But a general truce was apparent when, in time for the start of the 1929 tournament season, the LTA announced that nine other makes of ball had been added to their authorised and approved list including specific products of Dunlop, Slazenger, Ayres and Spalding. It was the start of an era of LTA approval being achieved by strict adherence to technical and performance criteria, and continuous and close co-operation between the Association and manufacturers to ensure that ball quality and development is in tune with the demands of the modern game.

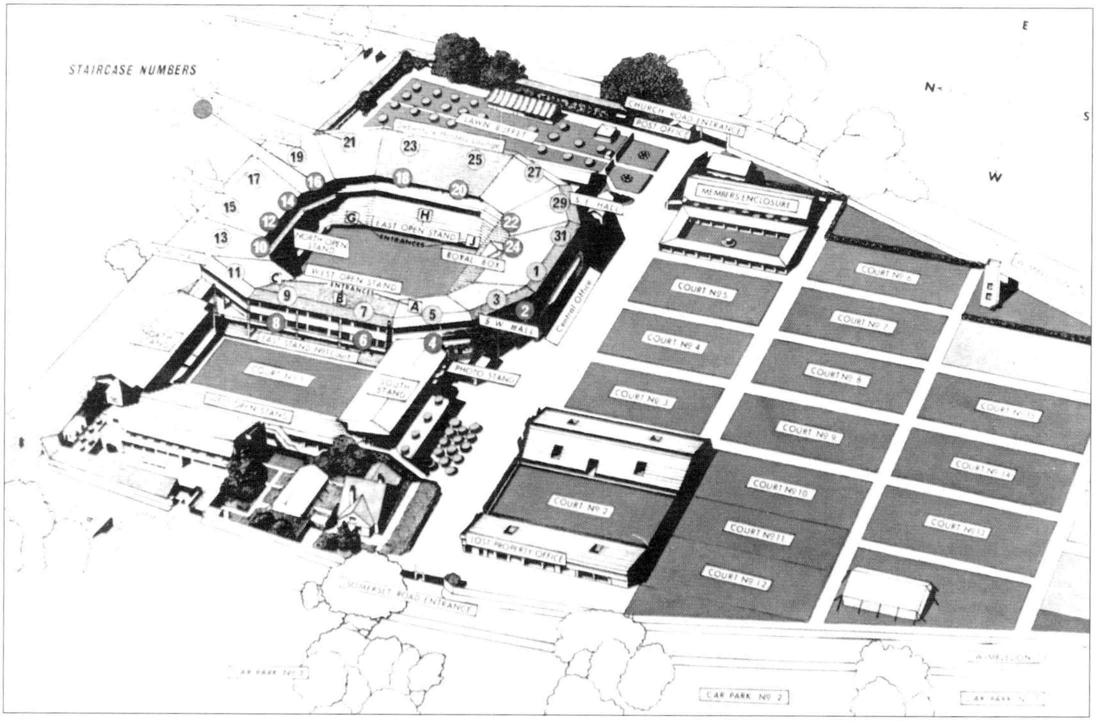

Lay-out of the All England club courts at Wimbledon where the world tennis championships were resumed in 1946 – with Slazenger balls.

Britain was entering an Economic Crisis, a Depression, in which the Chancellor of the Exchequer fought to balance his budget, raised the standard rate of income tax to five shillings (25 pence) in the £, and in September 1931 hurriedly suspended the operation of the gold standard. The departure from sterling was resisted to the uttermost, but it brought relief to British finance and industry. To steer Britain through the economic blizzard, the political parties joined forces in a National Government.

WELL ABLE TO SURVIVE THE DEPRESSION AFTER 50 YEARS

It was the year in which Slazenger celebrated their Golden Jubilee, 1881-1931. The special supplement in *Sports Dealer* pinpointed the very different circumstances in which the sports trade operated in the 1930s compared with the times when Ralph and Albert launched their enterprise.

> In the past, orders flowed in as a matter of course, and there was little need to search for work. Now times are changing; the days of relying on reputation have passed, and although Slazenger have always been first choice where quality is the supreme test, the question of price must also be considered, particularly in these difficult times.

Their difficulties not only reflected the depressed state of the world economy, but the growing strength of competition for the supply of sports equipment at home and abroad. However, as a result of meticulously building up their business step by step over 50 years, Slazenger operated on a firm base, well able to withstand whatever assailed them. In 1931 they employed 670, of whom 566 were engaged in manufacture. Their welfare was a

Vive le sport! The branch which Slazenger opened in the French capital controlled the Sporting Club de Paris.

major concern of Albert Slazenger who made them a present of six hard and four grass tennis courts at a recreation centre in Eltham, which also sported a football field and a cricket pitch.

In 1926 the company had acquired a second factory in Great Alie Street, a short distance from their Cannon Street offices, equipped with all the latest machinery for economising time and labour, to supplement production at Woolwich. When it came to marketing their output, there had never been any question of the directors accepting the idea that first class goods sold themselves. For that reason, they had, very early on, set up agencies in Australia and Canada, which had become locally registered manufacturing and

William Sykes 1903 advert for their 'E.D.B.' rackets.

An 1890 advertisement of H Gradidge of Woolwich – 'All Tennis Bats Strung with Best English Gut'.

marketing operations. The branch they established in the French capital controlled the Sporting Club de Paris.

The outlets were plentiful; it was a matter of maintaining the flow of products to them before the competition grew any larger and the name 'Slazenger' began losing its pre-eminence. When, in 1931, the opportunity came to expand the business, they grabbed it.

FROM 1931, IN ALLIANCE WITH GRADIDGES

Harry Gradidge started making cricket bats in Artillery Place, Woolwich, in 1870, and had cricket balls made for him by one of the many manufacturers in Tonbridge. He soon saw the wisdom of making his own, took a small workshop in an upper room at 149a High Street, Tonbridge, and became a keen member of the Cricket Ball Manufacturers' Association. As such, he became involved in the same situation as the one in which the LTA found itself in relation to the tennis ball makers. He complained that Wisden had supplied balls direct to the MCC at a price lower than agreed by the Association – 108s a dozen. Wisden had to agree that was the case, but they had made an error which they would not repeat.

In 1927, Harry's son Henry (Tim) Gradidge died, and H Gradidge & Son, with its now much larger factory in Woolwich, makers of a very much wider range of sports goods than cricket

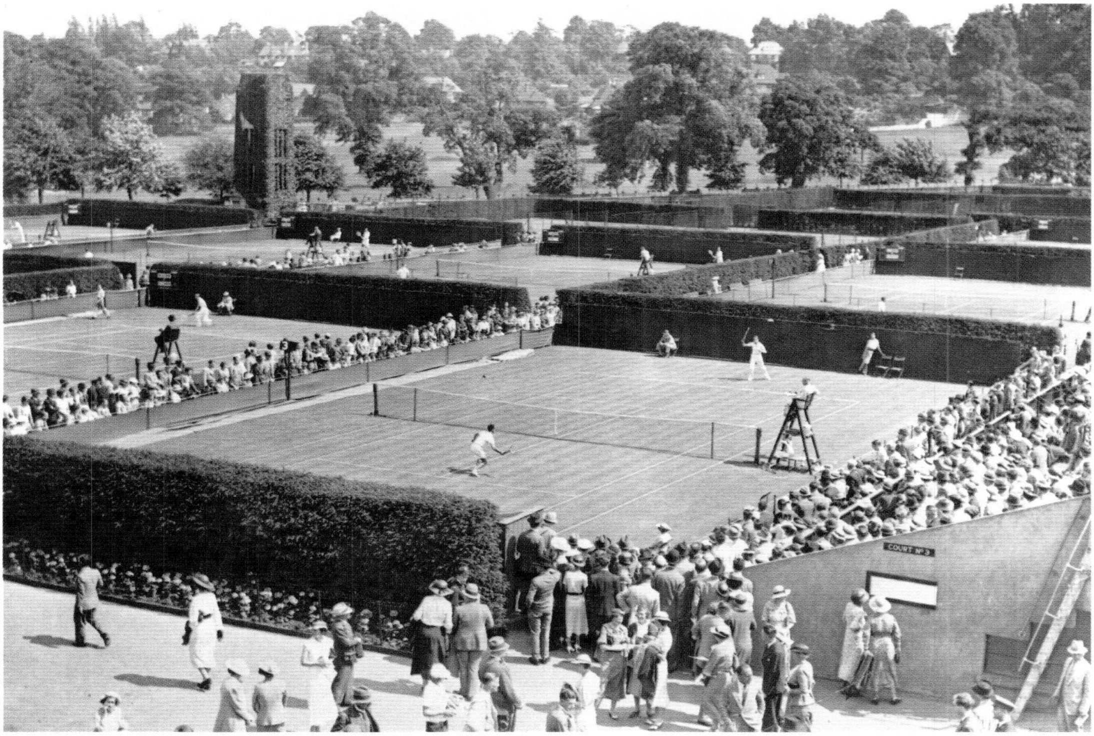

How easy to walk about the outside courts in the 1930s.

bats and balls, were bought by Humphrey McMaster, a scratch golfer who had won the South African amateur title, and his twin brother Michael McMaster, also an accomplished sportsman. Aged 31, they came from Porlock in Somerset. 'Although they have not been in Woolwich very long,' commented *Sports Trader* reporting the opening of an extension to the Woolwich works in 1930, 'the McMasters have proved themselves real good sportsmen, young men of initiative and enterprise, and to be trusted to continue the fine traditions of the House of Gradidge.'

They did not choose to do so on their own. The following year, Humphrey and Michael McMaster approached Archdale Palmer and Tim Hadingham, who now partnered him as joint managing director of Slazenger, with the suggestion that they bought Gradidges from them. The two managing directors consulted Albert Slazenger and other members of the board, who instructed them to go ahead and negotiate a deal.

From 1931, therefore, Slazengers owned Gradidges, but what the two firms negotiated was more of an alliance than a merger. Gradidges continued to operate separately – with its own brands and expertise. And a very successful alliance it proved. Among those to later use Slazenger/Gradidge products were the cricketing 'greats' Len Hutton, Denis Compton, Gary Sobers and Colin Cowdrey – as well as many of today's leading players – and also legendary winners of many major golf championships like Bobby Locke, Jack Nicklaus, Johnny Miller and Seve Ballesteros.

The popularity of tennis in the 1930s, and the demand for Slazenger rackets and balls, owed a great deal to Britain's eight times Grand Slam champion Fred Perry, seen here being carried along the platform of London's Victoria Station on his return from Britain's Davis Cup victory in Paris in 1933.

3. Four-Hand Drive

WITH their flourishing overseas business combining export to a worldwide network of distributors and their own operations in the dominions and colonies, the Slazenger Gradidge alliance was, in the 1930s, the most prominent sports business in the UK, with tennis still the main field of activity. In their catalogue Slazenger showed a range of 23 tennis rackets.

When Fred Perry won Wimbledon in 1934, he was the first Briton to do so since Arthur Gore's victories of 1908 and 1909. He made it known in 1939 that he had used no other racket than one made by Slazenger for seven years, and that all his major successes had been achieved with their aid – not only at Wimbledon (in 1934, 1935 and 1936) but in the USA, France and Australia. He told the company that he had decided to have an autograph racket made, 'and since Slazengers make the best in the world, I am writing to ask you to produce a "Fred Perry" racket for me'. The racket, bearing the Fred Perry name selling at £3 15s, was available alongside the ever popular 'Doherty', 'Demon', 'Victory' and 'Queens' models. A repair and re-stringing service was introduced, with 36 variations of gut in white, red, green, black, plain orange or orange with dark blue. Slazenger tennis balls were adopted not only by the All England club for Wimbledon, but by 112 other tournaments in Britain and 81 principal overseas championships. For players in tropical climates, the balls were packed in compressed air tins. To keep the sun out of their eyes, players in any climate could buy the company's 'Tally-Ho' and 'Yoicks' sports hats and visors; and for their feet 'Fred Perry' tennis shoes.

Tennis was enjoying enormous worldwide popularity, and nowhere more so than in Britain where watching and playing the game was driven by Fred Perry's eight Grand Slam titles in only four years, as well as his 45 wins out of 52 matches, during Britain's four year period of Davis Cup supremacy. Slazenger were reaping the rewards of the energy and vision of Ralph and Albert, and the management and marketing skills of Archdale Palmer, Humphrey and Michael McMaster, Tim Hadingham and his son Reginald (Buzzer) who joined the company in 1933.

It was all too good to last. In 1939, for the second time in 20 years, the men and women of Britain were mobilised for 'active service' on the home front and overseas. The outbreak of the Second World War hit Slazenger, as it did so many other enterprises, very hard. Their profit for the year ending December 1939 was down to £27,279. In the first few months of the war, production levels significantly increased, since the Government encouraged export sales to pay for vitally needed imports, but it was the lull before the storm. In June 1940 Albert Slazenger died at the age of 84, after nearly 60 years at the helm of the now internationally famous family business, in the success of which he had played so prominent a part.

Managers, factory workers, office and sales staff joined the armed forces, including Humphrey McMaster who in 1941 enlisted in the Royal Canadian navy. His brother Michael took over as managing director, with the support of Ralph Slazenger, Albert's son, who, although the major shareholder, did not wish to become heavily involved in its management. European sales manager 'Buzzer' Hadingham left to serve in the army. The trading profit dropped from £20,000 in 1941 to £14,456 in 1942, although by 1944 it had recovered to almost £25,000.

Their main factory at Woolwich was almost completely destroyed in a German incendiary raid, along with most of its stock of products. The nearby Gradidge works were badly damaged in the same raid. As a result, Slazenger's total production capacity was enormously reduced. Limited tennis ball production was organised at the Old Brewery, Hurstpierpoint, in Sussex. They later acquired another factory in High Wycombe where they contributed to the war effort by producing and repairing aircraft airframes and wings.

In 1940, two of the sports trade's largest operators, and Slazenger's major competitors, amalgamated: William Sykes Limited and F H Ayres.

The former had been founded by William Sykes in 1870 in Horbury near Leeds where they built the huge Yorkshire Athletic Manufactory. By the time William died in 1910, his firm had become the largest sports equipment manufacturers in the UK, perhaps the world. It grew from the saddlery which, at the age of 23, William bought in Horbury for £19, and there applied his leather-making skills to the making of

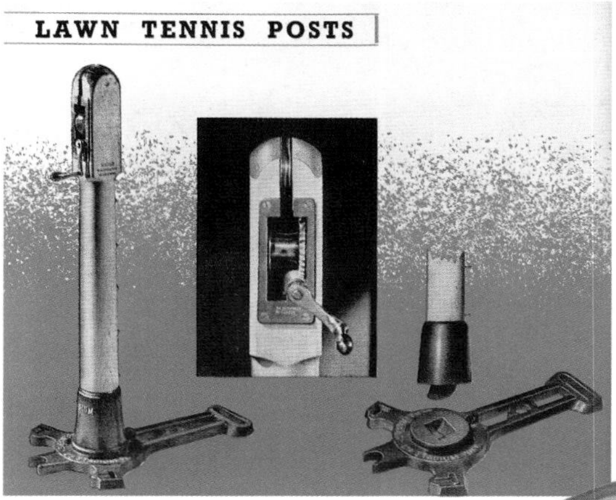

Slazenger provided Wimbledon with every kind of court furniture, such as the strong, reliable net posts.

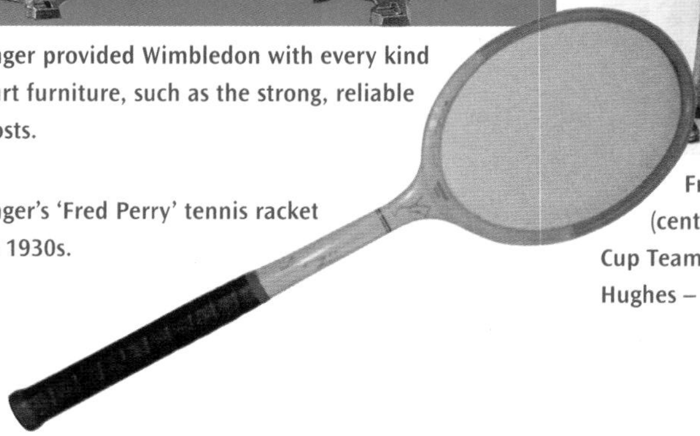

Slazenger's 'Fred Perry' tennis racket of the 1930s.

Fred Perry (second from left) beside Roper Barrett (centre) with other members of the victorious Davis Cup Team – Raymond Tuckey, 'Bunny' Austin and Pat Hughes – admire the trophy at Wimbledon in 1934.

footballs, then to leather-covered cricket balls, then cricket bats and tennis rackets. He was joined by his two sons, Henry and William, and was soon involved across the whole spectrum of sports equipment. Their premium tennis racket the 'EDB', was made for E D Black, tennis champion of Yorkshire, one of more than 20 models. Their tennis range, including the premium 'Electric' tennis ball, provided every item required for setting up a court and for a player's use. Far and away the most famous of the sportsmen who used Sykes equipment was the world's greatest cricketer, Donald Bradman, who chose one of their bats as a gift from his mother when he was only 17 and used Horbury-made products for most of his career.

The firm of F H Ayres had sprung from the cabinet making business which Edward Ayres had started in Clerkenwell in 1810. It had become a very substantial sports equipment manufacturer and offered, as one of its first tennis products, canvas 'wells' in which the balls were kept at the side of the court. These, they claimed, were 'indispensable to every lawn tennis court, by which stooping for balls was avoided and the game not interrupted'.

Ayres, too, had marketed a large range of tennis rackets and for many years had been major suppliers of tennis balls, which, as seen, had included providing balls for Wimbledon over 22 years, from 1879, which was two years before the foundation of the Slazenger business in Manchester.

Albert Slazenger, who died in June 1940 at the age of 84.

SLAZENGER-GRADIDGE ACQUIRED SYKES-AYRES TO FORM 'FAMOUS FOUR'

In wartime, the market for sports goods inevitably declined, and these pioneering sports traders, both slimmer than they were used to being, saw the commercial sense of being more likely to survive those difficult times and be able to develop after them, in partnership rather than rivalry.

Following a train conversation, between Michael McMaster, managing director of Slazenger, and Bill Dunning, his counterpart in the newly merged William Sykes Ayres business, negotiations began two years later for a further Slazenger/Gradidge-Sykes/ Ayres amalgamation. It cost Slazenger's Ltd, in 1942, £149,270. In the consolidated balance sheet for that year, the 'Famous Four' Slazenger-Gradidge-Sykes-Ayres Group was valued at £348,500, which included £45,622 for Slazenger Australia and £10,688 for their Canadian business.

The overall approach was to combine the London based and mainly Slazenger and

Gradidge marketing expertise, brand strength and strong financial position, which was suddenly faced with the wartime loss of most of its production capacity, with the manufacturing strength of Sykes crucially located in relatively safe Yorkshire. For the time being the Horbury factory was fully occupied with orders from the Ministry of Defence, but the new group management could at least begin to plan their strategy for when peace came.

With the start, in 1945, of a new era, after Victory in Europe and then the Far East, the 'Famous Four' pledged 'worthily to uphold the tradition of British craftsmanship and manufacturing skill in the age of Reconstruction', and so help foster not only British industry and commerce but also the worldwide Fellowship of Sport 'through which so much can be done to promote peace and reconciliation among the nations in the years to come'. They resumed full production at Horbury, moved their tennis ball operation to a newly acquired factory at Barnsley and closed Gradidge's Woolwich factory. The four companies were now fully fused under the three executive directors Michael and Humphrey

Below: Williams Sykes Ltd's extensive factory at Horbury near Leeds which is where the 'Famous Four' tennis rackets were made after World War 2.
Left: The ladies pose at a Slazenger gala day in the 1950s.

McMaster and Bill Dunning (who died in 1948). The senior sales managers were in London, the manufacturing and operating managers at Horbury. Norman Groves went from London to Barnsley to set up the new tennis ball operation. The Slazenger brand quickly became the prime promotional focus, with the accent on tennis and Fred Perry, and it was also used as the corporate link for the other brands. It was a winning strategy. Trading profit for 1945 at £28,332 was double that of 1942.

WIMBLEDON CHAMPIONSHIPS, ON HOLD DURING WAR, RESUME IN 1946

The first Wimbledon lawn tennis championships after the Second World War were held in the traditional fortnight of 1946, once again with Slazenger balls. The first of the company's many post-war tournament sponsorships was the Scarborough Professional Tennis Tournament which offered £700 prize money and another £300 for players' expenses. The winner, Dan Maskell, received a challenge trophy and 200 guineas. Slazenger gave the tennis racket range a new flagship frame in 1953, the 'Slazenger I.C.' at seven guineas (£7 7s) with an individual registration number which allowed the purchaser to replace it with an exact match; and also the Perry/Maskell Instructional Racket. It was the year they introduced 'Paddle Tennis' played with wooden bats on a court, hard or soft, measuring 39 x 18ft, for which they offered a complete set for just over £7 comprising posts, bats, balls and rule book. In spite of the Paddle Tennis Association formed to promote it, the game never caught on in Britain but was popular in South America.

If the company, of which Ralph Slazenger

Dan Maskell, who won, with his Slazenger racket, the first tennis tournament for professionals staged by the company in 1946.

1960s Wimbledon – this photo showing a different type of service to commemorate the 75th Anniversary of the diocese of Southwark.

LEFT: Fred Perry.

ABOVE: Dorothy Chambers.

BELOW LEFT: 'Bunny' Austin.

BELOW: Althea Gibson receiving the doubles championship trophy from H.R.H. The Duchess of Kent. On the left is her partner Darlene Hard.

FACING PAGE

MAIN PICTURE: Manuel Orantes.

CENTRE: Ken Rosewall.

BELOW: Neale Fraser.

ABOVE LEFT: Jimmy Connors.

ABOVE: Tim Henman.

LEFT: Bjorn Borg as a Junior.

PREVIOUS PAGE

MAIN PICTURE: John Newcombe.

CENTRE: Margaret Court.

BELOW: Christine Truman.

Some of the Slazenger Tennis Greats – past and present

was still the major shareholder, was to continue to grow in the increasingly competitive market, it would need a considerable and sustained level of investment. Its established marketing strength would become increasingly expensive to maintain, and it was thought unlikely that Ralph would be prepared to underwrite such a future. How better to obtain the money than by putting the shares on the market at a time when their value was high? In 1957, gross profit before tax and interest passed £250,000 for the first time. The company asked shareholders not to dispose of their holdings since discussions were taking place with a firm of 'the highest standing' which was interested in acquiring the issued Ordinary capital, currently quoted at 8s 6d a share – costing the purchaser a sum in the region of £1 million. Ralph Slazenger had his own idea about a purchaser and was in the USA talking to Wilson, one of America's largest sports equipment companies. But at a Slazenger board meeting in December 1958, the directors considered the offer they had received from The Dunlop Rubber Company based on an exchange of ten Slazenger Ordinary 5s shares for six Dunlop Ordinary 10s stock units. On the recommendation of the board, more than 90 per cent of Slazenger shareholders accepted the offer, and in 1959, after 77 years, the business started by Ralph and Albert Slazenger in Manchester ceased to be independent and became part of the worldwide Dunlop empire, although it was agreed that Slazenger should operate separately in the sports market place. The products of the Dunlop Sports Division and those of Slazenger would all be sold in competition. However, they emphasised the two companies had common aims as regards the promotion and welfare of sport and the protection of the legitimate trade.

AMALGAMATION, BUT STILL COMPETITION, WITH DUNLOP FROM 1959

From the Slazenger point of view, the picture for most of the 20 years following amalgamation with Dunlop was one of a sturdily independent operation. The company had its own board of directors, which included

at least one and sometimes two Dunlop representatives, one always the current general manager of the Dunlop Sports Company. Michael McMaster remained chairman and managing director until 1965, when he was succeeded by his brother Humphrey. When the Laurence Pountney Hill offices, which they had occupied since 1883, were demolished in 1962 to make way for the extension of the Victoria Embankment, they moved to a new head office at Challenge House, Croydon. In the same year they set up Slazenger Inc as a first step in building a significant presence in the USA. Two years later, they became part of The International Sports Company Ltd which Dunlop created in 1964, with George Carr as general manager, to operate as the controlling company for all their interests in sport within

Fast reaction before service and steadfast immobility after it was demanded from every Wimbledon ball boy and girl assembled opposite for a group photograph – and if the call finds you empty-handed, the signal is this.

the UK. Its major British manufacturing units were at Horbury, Barnsley, Speke (golf balls), Waltham Abbey (Dunlop 'Maxply' tennis rackets) and Glasgow (golf clubs).

During the next few years the combined resources of Dunlop and Slazenger worked on the development of first the steel and then the graphite frames that would spell the end of the wooden racket, on pressureless tennis balls with nearly all the resilience of a pressurized ball, and new tennis ball cloth with material made from a needled Nylon-wool mixture with improved wearing properties.

Sports clothing, with the new Slazenger 'panther' logo, assumed greater and greater importance in the product line in the 1970s and 1980s and in 1977 the company became distributors of the 'Puma' sports footwear range in the UK. The extra visibility of the panther logo on the clothing line, particularly on the famous V-necked sweater, was increased by ensuring that panther-emblazoned sportswear was worn not only by leading players but also by show business personalities such as Sean Connery, Harry Secombe, Bruce Forsyth and Max Bygraves.

Throughout all these changes, Slazenger's tie with Wimbledon remained in the ascendant. With the appointment of 'Buzzer' Hadingham as managing director in 1973, a post his father had held from 1920 to 1937 and two years later taking over from Humphrey McMaster as chairman, the link was stronger than ever. Buzzer had been a member of the All England Lawn Tennis Club since 1957; was chairman from 1983 to 1989 and remains a vice-president.

Dunlop and Slazenger had separate sponsorship programmes, with different players endorsing the leading products. Competition between the two businesses was sufficiently strong to result in several players being enticed from one to the other by a better deal. On one occasion a last minute decision by the Dunlop main Board resulted in John McEnroe's tennis racket carrying the Dunlop 'Flying D' logo instead of the Slazenger panther.

The last 25 years of Slazenger's existence as a separate operation, albeit wholly owned by Dunlop, proved as dramatic as anything that had gone before, set against the background of a sports market place that experienced its greatest upheaval since the explosion of popular interest in outdoor leisure pursuits 100 years earlier. Both Dunlop and Slazenger brands flourished spectacularly enough to be seen as dominant in tennis. Dunlop or Slazenger rackets won 80 out of the 112 men's and women's Grand Slam tennis titles contested between 1960 and 1973, 38 of them going to Slazenger, most of them to Margaret Court, John Newcombe and Ken Rosewall. This period of shared supremacy in their main sports of tennis and golf was not maintained during the remaining ten years of the separate Slazenger operation, since the market place was becoming more and more competitive both in terms of overseas-based new entrants, and the generally more aggressive promotional investment.

In 1985 Slazenger ceased to exist as a completely separate company when, shortly after the Dunlop Rubber Company had been taken over by British Thermoplastics and Rubber (BTR), it became an important part of the newly-formed Dunlop Slazenger Limited, which was given the responsibility for the development of all sports operations in Europe, North America and the Far East. During the following ten years this business more than doubled in size and was the basis of the 1996 Management Buy Out from BTR to form today's Dunlop Slazenger International Limited.

Throughout all of these changes and, of course, during the previous 120 years, the Slazenger name has been, first and foremost, associated with tennis. And at the core of this tennis focus has been the 100-year relationship with Wimbledon. In terms of the main products Slazenger and Ayres rackets have won more singles titles at Worple Road and Church Road than any other manufacturer and their balls have been used for all but the first two years of the tournament – Slazenger's for the last 100 years – which is a quite unique record in the history of the game.

The very first Men's champion, Spencer Gore, used an Ayres racket and the 100% Slazenger/Ayres winning streak from 1896 to 1919 was dominated by the Doherty brothers, Laurie and Reginald, Arthur Gore and the Australian, Tony Wilding. Fred Perry was the champion for three years from 1934 to 1936 and, after the Second World War, Neale Fraser, Ken Rosewall, Roy Emerson, Manuel Santana and John Newcombe were prominent among the leading men, and Althea Gibson, Margaret Smith, Christine Truman, Betty Stove and Sue Barker among the ladies.

In recent years Tim Henman has carried British hopes and played brilliant tennis, now also on clay, despite the huge pressure of a nation's expectations. If anything, that pressure has been even greater in Jubilee Year because Tim has been so successful in consolidating his position in the world's top ten players. He is playing with the Slazenger Pro Braided racket, developed by the company's technical staff with his close collaboration.

HELPING TO RUN WIMBLEDON

The number of balls supplied for the championships, not unexpectedly, has greatly increased since that fifteen dozen provided by Jefferies and Company in 1877. As the tournament has grown in terms of numbers of competitors, prize money and the facilities for both the players and the hundreds of thousands of spectators, so the number of balls required for the qualifying stages, practice and for the championship matches has multiplied many times over. Now, 4150 dozen are supplied, every one carefully tested and inspected before leaving the factory. New balls are required after the first seven games – to allow for the warm-up – and then after every nine games. The yellow balls now in general use replaced the original white balls in 1986 and the 2002 tournament sees the introduction of the 'Ultra Vis' ball with its unique 'Hydroguard' water-resistant cover.

Testing the humidity of the court to make sure it's fit to play.

RV
Slazenger
SCOREBOARD TELEPHONE

Modern Wimbledon with Slazenger on the chair.

Setting the stage.

Slazenger is the only manufacturer to have supplied balls to all four of the Grand Slam tournaments – the US, Australian and French Open championships as well as Wimbledon.

However, the very special Slazenger association with Wimbledon goes a long way beyond delivering nearly 50,000 perfect balls and designing winning rackets. Because tennis has always been so important for the company, it invested heavily in sponsoring and supporting many of the major tournaments in the UK and set up a tournament department for this purpose. Very few of the thousands that throng the championships every year realise just how much of what they see around the courts has been put in place by this department. A winter visitor to Wimbledon might, for instance, be surprised to see the large open spaces of grass which in June divide into a complex pattern of courts, spectator walkways, temporary stands and marquees.

Indeed, not so many years ago, and before the All England club had increased its staff, more than a dozen Slazenger employees were on duty every Wimbledon fortnight not only responsible for the company's equipment and clothing, but also fulfilling important roles within the total operation. They worked in the Referee's Office, helping to make sure each day's programme was completed without delays, had special responsibilities looking after the key matches on the Centre and Number One courts, and were also responsible for the players' transport arrangements.

There is a wonderful (and true!) story that the club secretary forgot to order the balls and woke up in a panic on the morning of the tournament. Happily Slazenger had assumed the order and the balls duly arrived.

However, their most important role has

always been the work of the equipment staff and this continues to the present day. The task is formidable. With the team also building the court surrounds at the qualifying tournament held at the Bank of England club, at Roehampton, everything must be absolutely perfect. The preparation for one year starts almost immediately the equipment for the previous year has been dismantled. All the metalwork used to erect the courts – nearly 1400 stakes and rods ranging from 3 to 8 feet – is repainted and the 70,000 square feet of heavy canvas sheeting surrounding the courts and marking the walkways is repaired or, if necessary, renewed.

It takes around 120 tons of wood, metal and canvas to set up the courts for the qualifying and main tournaments. This includes 60 nets, 40 pairs of posts, 22 umpire's chairs, 27 hand-operated scoreboards, 2000 yards of stop netting and 3000 yards of polypropylene rope – as well as the stakes, rods and canvas. The team builds the surrounds for the 20 courts required for the main tournament, all with different dimensions and requirements – for instance, in 2001 the Centre Court surrounds had to be adjusted to accommodate a new TV camera. A team of seven men work flat out for six weeks before the first Monday of the championships to get everything ready, and it takes three weeks to take everything down again. During the fortnight the team is virtually on 24 hour standby to deal with any problems and one or more helpers can always be found in their 'Operations Room' tucked away in a corner behind the private marquees in the southern corner of the grounds.

For over 120 years Wimbledon has provided the stage for so much tennis drama, so many epic contests to thrill many millions of spectators in the grounds and via TV. For the last 100 years Slazenger has been very proud to play its important supporting role. Truly Friends at Court.

Slazenger® OFFICIAL BALL TO WIMBLEDON 1902-2002

THE CHAMPIONSHIPS WIMBLEDON

For further information contact:
Dunlop Slazenger International Ltd
Carrgate, Wakefield, North Yorkshire WF2 0XB
www.slazenger.com